Hard Disk Management for the IBM PC XT, AT, and Compatible Systems

Hard Disk Management
for the IBM PC XT, AT and
Compatible Systems

Thomas Cain

The Dun & Bradstreet Corporation

Nancy Woodard Cain

Morgan Guaranty Trust Company

A Brady Book
Published by Prentice Hall Press
New York, New York 10023

Hard Disk Management for the IBM PC XT, AT, and Compatible Systems

A Brady Book
Published by Prentice Hall Press
A Division of Simon & Schuster, Inc.
Gulf + Western Building
One Gulf + Western Plaza
New York, New York 10023

PRENTICE HALL PRESS is a trademark of Simon & Schuster, Inc.

Designed by Michael O'Brien
Manufactured in the United States of America

 3   4   5   6   7   8   9   10

Library of Congress Cataloging-in-Publication Data

Cain, Thomas.
  Hard disk management.

  Includes index.
  1. IBM microcomputers—Programming.   2. File
organization (Computer science)   3. Magnetic disks.
I. Cain, Nancy Woodard.   II. Title.
QA76.8.I2594C34   1986   005.74   85-28672

ISBN 0-89303-669-2 (Paper Edition)

To Our Mothers

Contents

Preface

This book is a guide to managing fixed disk systems. Three categories of end-users will find it particularly useful:

1. The first-time XT or AT user.
2. The experienced PC user who is a first-time XT or AT user.
3. The experienced XT or AT user who wants to better manage his/her resource.

This book draws upon the authors' experiences as end-user computing professionals. The perspective taken throughout this book reflects the authors' managerial concerns as non-programming users of hard disk systems.

For the first-time XT or AT user, this book provides an introduction to the XT/AT hardware and operating system. It then takes the user through the essentials of DOS, demonstrating the usefulness of DOS's commands to users of all levels.

Experienced XT and AT users will find numerous ideas and examples to make their systems more efficient and secure. These include an introduction to filenaming conventions; the advantages of and techniques for creating a menu system; a discussion of security-related procedures and options; and issues that one must address when looking ahead to networking.

Many individuals provided ideas and the motivation required to produce a book such as this. The authors particularly would like to thank Bill Carpenter, Mike Miller of DunsNet, and Marcel Malenfant of Morgan for their critical reviews and commentary on the manuscript. Erika Cowan of Morgan deserves special mention for contributing many ideas and, in particular, for her insight into the world of filenaming conventions. Daniel Woodard has provided expert financial advice for several of our adventures.

Other individuals at D&B and Morgan deserve thanks as well: Jim Hanley, David Katz, Andy Lippa, Leonor Lopez, Judy Martin, and Michael Shipe.

DISCLAIMER STATEMENT

1.

Introduction

A microcomputer, like any other business resource, needs to be managed. This is particularly true for the XT, AT, and other hard disk systems. Armed with some basic knowledge of the system and DOS commands, routines can be developed that allow the *user* to control the system. For example, one can "paint" colored logo screens, automate the backing up of a data-filled disk, and create a menu system that organizes information on the disk—all using DOS. One does not have to be a programmer to access DOS's hidden powers, nor does one have to invest a penny—just a little time and patience.

This chapter describes the approach that this book takes to presenting DOS, emphasizing the user's perspective. It also discusses what is meant by "managing" a hard disk system and why a hard disk system must be managed. Both topics set the scene for the remainder of the book: How various techniques can be applied to get the most out of an XT or AT system. This information is followed by a brief description of each chapter.

1.1. DOS through the Eyes of the User

To the non-programmer, DOS seems vast. It comes with a fat, mysteriously organized manual that appears to contain trillions of commands. One wonders what the connection is between all of this information and the daily operation of the XT or AT. On the other hand, the user of a hard disk system finds it difficult (if not impossible) to ignore DOS. The very nature of a hard disk system forces the user into some acknowledgement of DOS.

This book does not take the approach that the AT or XT user must know everything about DOS. For business users, knowing DOS should not be simply an end in itself; having a knowledge of DOS simply for the sake of that knowledge is for hackers, tinkerers, and other individuals whose job it is to discover how things work. This book presents only those aspects of DOS that are useful in running an XT or AT system on a day-to-day basis. Information about DOS is presented in a context that clarifies both its significance and its utility for the hard disk user.

1

The DOS Information in This Book

The information about DOS in this book falls into two general categories: 1) information about specific DOS commands, and 2) techniques and circumstances for using these commands. The DOS commands that are discussed relate to the organization, storage, retrieval, and protection of data stored on a hard disk system. The commands are presented from a user perspective, with specific situations describing how and why the command is used.

The user also will find that the DOS-related techniques described in this book will make life with an XT or an AT considerably easier. Specific routines are described that allow a user to automate DOS operations. This automated processing of DOS operations can be of immense value:

- Automated routines can simplify complicated processes for the less knowledgeable
- Repetitive tasks can be done by the system instead of the user
- Multiple tasks can be accomplished in one operation

This automated processing can be taken one step further. Techniques for developing a menu-driven system for DOS functions are described in detail.

In describing a particular command or DOS routine, a step-by-step approach is taken. There is a generous use of example screens for each given situation.

The DOS information explored in this book ranges from basic to reasonably sophisticated. However, at all levels, the intent is to present the non-programming reader with DOS information that can be of use in managing a hard disk system.

1.2. Why Manage a Hard Disk System?

Managing a hard disk system means *PLANNING* for its use, *CONTROLLING* the integrity of the system, and *ORGANIZING* the structure of its storage media. As such, a hard disk system is just another tool used by the business manager. It allows the manager to perform a number of manual tasks more accurately and efficiently. When managed well, a hard disk system can result in substantial cost savings and higher quality services.

Hard disk systems such as the XT and the AT allow the user to electronically store massive amounts of information and to retrieve that information in a matter of seconds. In addition, large complex applications that were too large or cumbersome for the PC can be handled with ease by the XT or AT.

Thus, more and more PC users are finding that they require the increased capacity of a hard disk system.

A hard disk system must be managed carefully. For example, a disorganized system can make a poorly labeled file extraordinarily difficult to find. Failure to backup the hard disk can mean the potential loss of thousands of files and thousands of hours lost in recovery time. Or a system that is understandable to only one individual can produce a severe bottleneck in processing time. Managing a hard disk system is *making it work for the user—* gaining control over the system rather than being at its mercy.

Planning a Hard Disk System

Planning a hard disk system means establishing a system that can be accessed by users of all skill levels. It also means establishing a system that allows new applications to be added, and one that anticipates the need to proactively organize data files. Planning a hard disk system, therefore, is not unlike establishing a library: It must be layed out in a logical and consistent fashion; it must be designed with enough space to grow (and potentially diversify); and it must have a filing scheme that permits librarians to shelve new or returned books into preestablished places (e.g., the Dewey Decimal system).

Imagine how frustrating it would be to look for a book in a library that permitted borrowers to develop their own methods for filing titles. The same holds true for a hard disk system (even though microcomputer users seem to be a bit more tolerant). There is no doubt that the true efficiency and cost-effectiveness of microcomputer-based applications reside in the upfront planning of both the system *and* the applications.

Controlling the Integrity of a Hard Disk System

Controlling has two meanings to the hard disk system user: It means 1) ensuring that operations are performed correctly by authorized individuals, and 2) that the data in the system are securely maintained. Every hard disk user has his or her horror story about losing massive amounts of data to a slip of the fingers, a power outage, or to a malfunctioning hard disk. Possibly the worst story was that of the dentist who returned to his office to find that a thief had made off with his entire XT system (... and obviously the thief hadn't bothered to leave a copy of the data files).

Despite these stories, people are surprisingly lax about backing up their systems. One of the primary reasons is that the user is required to interact with DOS in order to back the system up efficiently. A well-managed hard disk system eliminates this excuse. No matter how well one has designed a spreadsheet application, it is only as good as the reliability of the data.

Organizing a Hard Disk System

Organizing a hard disk means establishing a logical framework within which to catalogue files. It also means ensuring that mechanisms are in place to keep this information neatly organized. Both elements of organization are essential components of the planning process described above.

Thousands of files may be stored on the XT or AT's hard disk. The user's ability to both identify the subjects of and easily retrieve these files depends on how well the fixed disk is organized. Files on a well-organized hard disk are grouped by application, by type, by user, and so on—by whatever structure makes the most sense in a particular organization. Logical groupings make life a lot easier when it comes time to "clean up" the hard disk.

The typical hard disk system user spends the majority of his or her time building files and manipulating data within files. However, a substantial portion of time also must be spent on housekeeping (i.e., moving files from one area of the disk to another, renaming files, combining files, and so on). Since the user is dealing with a fixed-capacity disk, he or she will periodically want to weed out seldom-used or duplicate files. If the user must examine each file to determine its contents and to whom it belongs, this process is even more inefficient. A well-organized hard disk permits users to identify the contents of files by their *filenames*. It also permits users to perform an operation on a number of files at the same time. The key to such efficiency is the proactive organization of data files.

1.3. Why Every Hard Disk System User Needs This Book

Managing a hard disk system is not an easy task. However, it is the key to making a microcomputer a truly efficient and reliable business resource.

A number of disk management techniques can be applied to hard disk systems. Conceptually, they are not difficult to apply. However, for the first-time XT or AT user the complexities of a hard disk system can be overwhelming. Even for an experienced PC user the conversion to a hard disk system can be difficult. This book does two things for these users: 1) It provides them with a thorough understanding of the system's capabilities, and 2) it introduces the user to various disk management concepts, while providing step-by-step, tested techniques for dealing with them.

By the time the user finishes with this book, DOS will no longer be a mystery. More importantly, the user will understand how DOS may be applied to better manage a hard disk system—how to make the system work for the user.

1.4. How This Book Is Organized

Much can be said about the management of a hard disk system. It can be a highly effective business tool for those who know how to tap its full capabilities. It is from this perspective that this book is written. The purpose of this book is twofold: 1) To familiarize the user with the operation of the XT and the AT, and 2) to raise managerial issues while providing creative solutions for them.

Chapter 2 describes the basics of the hardware and the operating system. Chapter 3 is an overview of disks, disk drives, and disk-related commands. Chapter 4 discusses all aspects of using a hierarchical directory system. Chapter 5 introduces the concepts of file management and maintenance.

Chapter 6, on filenaming conventions, provides the user with a tool for managing files efficiently. Chapters 7 and 8 discuss all aspects of batch files and what they can do for the user. Chapter 9 demonstrates the techniques required for creating a menu system and the rationale behind the techniques. Chapter 10 addresses the issue of data security and the options available to the user. Chapter 11, on PC networks, presents some information and terminology on networking, and the decision issues involved in selecting a PC network.

Chapter 12 ends the book by integrating these topics in a sample Menu Management System. Facts presented throughout the book come together to create some powerful tools that can be used to effectively manage your XT or AT System.

The Appendices contain the following information: How to enhance the system memory of an XT or AT (Appendix A); How to relocate an XT or AT (Appendix B); and a summary of EDLIN's basic commands (Appendix C).

2.

Hardware and Operating System Basics

This chapter introduces the reader to some fundamental terminology and information about the hardware and operating systems of the AT and XT. While going through this book, this information should give the reader the necessary framework with which to recognize the full potential of his or her system.

2.1. Some Basic Terminology

Data Storage

Information is stored by the computer in several different ways. One form of storage uses magnetic disks such as floppy diskettes and fixed disks. Both of these are for permanent data storage. (This subject is discussed separately in the next chapter.) Information also is stored in the computer in integrated circuits. Integrated circuits are used to store data on both a temporary and permanent basis. It is these integrated circuits that represent the computer's memory.

The integrated circuits that contain permanently stored data are known as ROM, which stands for *Read Only Memory*. ROM generally contains certain fundamental information that is used to run the computer. In the XT and AT, the BASIC interpreter is stored in ROM. The information stored in ROM can only be read by the computer; it cannot be changed.

The integrated circuits used for storing data on a temporary basis are known as *Random Access Memory*, which is abbreviated as RAM. RAM is used to store computer programs while they are being run, as well as other data used and created by the program or the user while the program is operating. RAM is available for data storage on a temporary basis (only while the computer is turned on). In order for the information stored in RAM to be saved permanently, it must be stored on a magnetic disk (e.g., the fixed disk). When users increase the size of the memory on their system it is most often the RAM memory that is increased.

Units of Data Storage

The amount of information that can be stored on disks and integrated circuits is measured in *bytes*. A byte is one character of information. A single letter or numeric character represents one byte. A larger unit of measurement that is commonly used to describe data storage capacity is a *kilobyte*. This represents 1,024 bytes. Although one might expect a kilobyte to contain 1,000 bytes, the actual value is a result of the binary mathematics that are used by the computer: The value 2 raised to the 10th power is 1,024. Kilobyte is frequently abbreviated to *K* or *KB*. For example, the storage capacity of a double-sided floppy diskette is roughly 360K, or 368,640 bytes.

An even larger unit of measure is a *megabyte*. This is abbreviated to *MB*. A megabyte represents 1,000 kilobytes or 1,024,000 bytes.

The size or capacity of an XT or AT is generally defined in terms of the amount of installed RAM. For example, someone might refer to his or her computer as a "512K machine." This means that this particular machine has 512 kilobytes of installed RAM. Until mid-1984, the XT included 128K of installed RAM as standard. After that date, this was increased to 256K. The Basic model of the AT has 256K of installed RAM; the Enhanced AT has 512K.

The Microprocessor(s)

The microprocessor or CPU (Central Processing Unit) in an XT or an AT is the single most important piece of hardware. It is the brain of the computer. It performs the calculations and controls the flow of information to the computer's other devices (video screen, printer, disk drives, and so on). For all of its importance, the microprocessor is a fairly small piece of equipment, measuring about one inch square. Figures 2–1 and 2–2 show the location of the microprocessor inside the system unit on both the XT and AT.

Discussions of microprocessors frequently will make use of another term that is a unit of measurement, the *bit*. A bit is an abbreviation for *binary digit*. It is the smallest unit of measurement in a computer, and it represents a single on or off switch. Eight bits constitute one byte. The processing power of microprocessors is defined in terms of bits, as in a "16-bit microprocessor." This means that the microprocessor can process 16 bits at a time.

The System Board

The main board in the system unit of the XT and AT is called the *system board* or *mother board*. It is the "floor" of the system unit. A large area of the system board is occupied by the RAM banks. Depending on the amount of installed RAM, these banks are filled either partially or completely. The remaining area of the system board contains the microprocessor, circuits for peripheral devices, and slots for expansion boards. Figures 2–1 and 2–2 show the system boards for the XT and AT.

Parallel and Serial Ports

The electrical connections between the system unit of an XT or AT and certain peripheral devices are called *interfaces*, and there are two types: *parallel* and *serial*. A parallel interface is used to connect the XT or AT to a parallel printer or plotter. A serial interface connects the XT or AT to serial printers, plotters, or modems. (Laser and letter-quality printers are usually serial devices, whereas dot-matrix printers are parallel devices.)

In order to use a parallel or serial device with the XT or AT, the system unit must contain a parallel or serial interface adapter card. The XT comes equipped with a serial interface adapter that is referred to as the *Asynchronous Communications Adapter Card*. The AT, on the other hand, comes with a single card that contains both serial and parallel interface adapters.

The jack into which the devices are plugged is often referred to as a *port*— a serial port or a parallel port. The easiest way to distinguish between the two different types of ports is by the type of plugs that each uses: Serial ports accept female plugs and parallel ports accept male plugs.

DOS distinguishes between the different interface adapters with certain reserved device names. The parallel ports are identified as *LPT1* or *LPT2* (for line printer #1 or #2). DOS also uses *PRN* to designate LPT1. The serial ports are designated as *COM1* or *COM2* (for communications device #1 or #2). Thus, DOS is capable of addressing two parallel devices (identified as LPT1 and LPT2) and two serial devices (identified as COM1 and COM2).

Figure 2–1. Photograph of XT system board, indicating the micro-processor ①, switch block ②, and memory banks ③.

Figure 2–2. Photograph of AT system board, indicating the microprocessor ① and memory banks ②.

The Operating System(s)

A disk operating system is a collection of programs through which the user communicates with his or her computer. These programs aid in the organization of data storage and control the reading and writing of data to and from disks. An operating system also controls how the computer interacts with application programs (programs such as Lotus 1-2-3, dBASE III, and DisplayWrite III).

The Personal Computer Disk Operating System (DOS) has been released in a number of versions: DOS 1.X was released with the PC, DOS 2.X with the XT, and DOS 3.X with the AT. Each new version provides additional features that aid in the organization and maintenance of a hard disk system.

Perhaps the most useful feature added to DOS's later versions (2.X and 3.X) was the inclusion of *hierarchical directories*. A directory contains a list of files stored on a disk along with reference information that tells DOS where each file is physically stored on the disk. Hierarchical directories refer to a disk structure in which directory entries contain names of lower-level directories, which in turn contain file names and their corresponding disk locations. This feature of DOS permits the user to store thousands of data files in an organized and systematic fashion.

2.2. Some Technical Aspects of the XT

The XT uses the same display and keyboard as the PC. The system unit is identical in size to that of the PC as well. In the spring of 1985, IBM announced that the XT would be sold with the fixed disk drive as optional. This means that an XT can now be purchased with one or two floppy disk drives and no hard disk.

However, for the purposes of this book, it is assumed that the XT contains a fixed disk drive. In this context, then, the basic hardware components of an XT system include a system unit with 256K memory, a 360KB floppy disk drive, a 10MB fixed disk, and an asynchronous communications adapter card. The floppy drive is located on the left side of the front panel; the fixed disk is located behind the right side. An indicator light on the front panel indicates when the fixed disk drive is in use.

Some of the internal characteristics of the XT are described below.

Expansion Slots in the XT

The XT comes with eight expansion slots for adapter cards, an improvement over the original PC, which has five. In actuality, the XT has five available slots because one is required for the display adapter card, one for the floppy drive controller card, and one for the fixed disk controller card. A fourth slot contains a half-length serial interface adapter card (for asynchronous communication) that is standard equipment with the XT. However, the asynchronous communications board is not critical to the XT's operation. Because eight slots are available in the same amount of space that the PC devotes to five slots, the XT's slots are more closely spaced. The two rightmost of the XT's expansion slots also may accommodate only half-length adapter cards because they are located behind the diskette drive.

The XT System Board

The system board of the XT contains a switch block that is labeled S–1. This switch block is a series of eight numbered, miniature on/off toggle switches. The configuration of a given XT must be reflected in the settings of these switches. They are used to indicate the amount of system board memory, the display type, the number of floppy drives, and the presence of the math coprocessor. The actual settings are described in the XT *Guide to Operations.*

The XT holds potentially 256K of Random Access Memory (RAM) on its system board. Each 64K of this memory is contained in a row of nine IC chips. A standard XT comes with 256K of RAM. A full system board contains four rows or banks of 64K chips. The amount of memory installed on the PC-XT is displayed in increments of 16K when the system is powered on.

Earlier versions of the XT came with 128K of RAM on the system board. If this is the case and the user wishes to increase the XT's RAM *above* 256K, the system board must first be brought up to 256K before expansion memory boards are added. The procedure for adding RAM to the system is described in Appendix A.

The XT Microprocessor

The XT's microprocessor is an Intel 8088. It is a 16-bit microprocessor, but it receives data from storage and sends results back eight bits at a time. The eight-bit limitation is a function of the 8088's eight-bit bus—eight channels or wires that link the microprocessor and the rest of the computer.

2.3. Some Technical Aspects of the AT

The AT comes in two models: The Basic AT (Model 68) and the Enhanced model (Model 99). The Basic AT comes with a single 1.2MB high-capacity floppy disk drive and 256K of RAM. The Enhanced model comes with a 20MB fixed disk drive, a 1.2MB high-capacity floppy drive, 512K of RAM, and a combination serial/parallel adapter card.

The only common part that the AT shares with the XT is the display. Otherwise, the AT has a different keyboard and system unit. Changes in the AT's keyboard, which is not compatible with other IBM micro models, include the addition of three LED mode indicators, enlarged SHIFT and ENTER keys, and the repositioning of some keys. The system unit itself is slightly larger than that of the PC and the XT. It is approximately two inches wider, one inch deeper, and one inch higher. The slight variations in size are required to accommodate the new 20MB fixed disk drive, space for two half-height floppy drives, and taller adapter cards. There is also a tubular lock on the front of the system unit that performs three functions: It disables the keyboard, prevents removal of the system unit cover, and prevents reinitialization of the system. Also evident on the front of the system unit are LED indicators for "power on" and fixed disk usage.

Unlike the XT, the AT accomodates half-height floppy disk drives (either 1.2MB or 360KB). These are located on the right side of the front panel. The top drive is typically a 1.2MB drive, whereas the bottom is either a 360KB drive or a second 20MB fixed disk. A fully "loaded" AT can accommodate two floppy disk drives and one fixed disk drive, or one floppy disk drive and two fixed disk drives. Thus, the AT can have direct access storage of up to 41.2MB.

The internal characteristics of the AT are described below.

Expansion Slots in the AT

The AT comes with eight expansion slots for adapter cards, which is the same as the XT. However, there is a more economical use of the slots in the AT. The functions of both the fixed disk controller and the floppy drive controller are combined into a single card. Another slot is occupied by the display adapter card. This means that there are six expansion slots available on the AT. A single synchronous/parallel input/output adapter card is standard on the Enhanced AT (Model 99). If this card is used, the number of available slots on the Enhanced AT is reduced to five.

All expansion slots will accommodate full-length cards.

The AT System Board

The AT's system board measures 12 inches by 13 inches. Unlike the XT and the PC, the AT no longer has switch blocks that are set by the user. Instead, the AT's system board contains two single switches: one to set the display as monochrome or color, and another to indicate either the presence or absence of a second 256K of RAM. In addition, the configuration of the system is "remembered" by a clock/calendar that is attached by wire to the system board. This clock/calendar is a Complementary Metal Oxide Semiconductor (CMOS) chip that is powered by a 6-volt lithium battery. The clock/calendar and system configuration (e.g., the amount of system and expansion RAM, the number of drives, the drive type, and so on) are set by using the AT's Diagnostic Disk at the time of system installation. To change the configuration at any time, the diagnostic disk is simply rerun.

The Basic AT and the Enhanced AT come with 256K of RAM and 512K of RAM, respectively. This memory is contained in 64K RAM chips, piggybacked into 128K of RAM. That is, the AT has four banks with nine pairs of chips in each bank; each chip has another chip on top of it. Thus, each bank is equal to 128K. All four banks are full on the Enhanced model. Only half of the banks are filled on the Basic AT.

The RAM of both AT models can be expanded to 3MB through the use of IBM's 128K and 512K memory expansion boards. The machine technically has the ability to use up to 16 MB of RAM using boards of other vendors.

The AT Microprocessor

The AT's microprocessor is an Intel 80286. This microprocessor processes information in 16 bits and has a 16-bit bus. It is a much more efficient and faster microprocessor than the XT's 8088 because of the 16-bit bus.

Unlike the XT's 8088 microprocessor, the AT's 80286 microprocessor is capable of supporting multiple users and multitasking. The key to this is the 80286's memory management capabilities, or the way in which it addresses memory. The 80286 can execute instructions stored:

1) As *REAL ADDRESSES* in which data, programs, etc. are stored as specific physical locations, or *addresses*, in memory. DOS 3.0, for example, operates in the *Real Address* mode only.
2) As *PROTECTED* or *VIRTUAL ADDRESSES* in which data are stored relative to some reference point; i.e., the physical location or address changes constantly depending on different programs, users, and so on.

2.4. An Overview of the Operating System

Recent releases of DOS provide many functions and features that can be invaluable aids in the use and maintenance of a hard disk system. DOS is more than a series of commands that control various aspects of file management. It also contains a number of features that allow the user to increase the flexibility of his or her system. An overview of some aspects common to both versions 2.X and 3.X of DOS is presented below.

Fixed Disk Partitions and Multiple Operating Systems

DOS allows the user to divide the fixed disk into four separate areas or *partitions*. Each of these partitions can contain a different operating system (i.e., operating systems different from DOS). These four partitions can vary in size; during installation, the user determines how much space to include in each partition by allocating parts of the fixed disk's cylinders (a *cylinder* is a unit of measurement on the fixed disk containing 34,816 bytes). DOS also gives the user the ability to specify the primary partition—the operating system that initially controls the computer when the system is turned on.

User-Created Configuration File

DOS allows the user to create a system configuration file. The contents of this file inform DOS how to structure various components of the system. That is, a configuration file permits the user to alter the computer's basic input/output system to fit his or her specific needs. When the computer is started or restarted, the configuration file is the first file read by DOS.

This configuration file is created by the user and is called CONFIG.SYS so that DOS will recognize it. One of the most useful functions of a CON-FIG.SYS file is to set the system's device drivers. A *device driver* is a hardware- or device-specific program to which DOS transfers control when it needs to access that hardware. For example, a device driver might be set to tell DOS how to control a graphics plotter. Device drivers also can be set to tell DOS how to modify many aspects of the video display. This topic is discussed in greater detail in Chapter 9.

Enhanced Screen and Keyboard Control

Using DOS commands with the appropriate device driver set in CON-FIG.SYS, the user can perform the following screen and keyboard operations:

1. Control the positioning of the cursor.
2. Erase the display.
3. Set various attributes of the display output such as brightness, the invisibility of characters, blinking characters, reverse video, and so on.
4. Change the colors of the display's foreground (color of the characters) and background (color of the screen). Eight colors may be set for each.
5. Reassign the meaning of any key (e.g., a command to initiate a system backup process can be set to be activated by the <F1> key.

The user also can redirect standard input and output to other devices. For example, the output that normally would appear on the display screen can be redirected to a file, a printer, or another peripheral such as a modem.

Control over the User Environment with DOS Commands

DOS includes a number of commands that allow the user to exercise considerable control over the way that files are stored and maintained on the fixed disk. Generally speaking, the major commands can be broken down into the following categories:

1. Disk Organization
   - MAKE DIRECTORY—creates a new directory or subdirectory
   - REMOVE DIRECTORY—removes a directory or subdirectory
   - CHANGE DIRECTORY—changes the current directory or subdirectory from one to another
   - SET SEARCH DIRECTORY (PATH)—defines the hierarchical structure or "path" of the directories and subdirectories to be searched for commands or files
   - DISPLAY DIRECTORY (TREE)—displays all hierarchical directory structures and/or lists files in each subdirectory
2. Batch File Commands (Batch files allow the user to string together one or more DOS commands into an executable file; i.e., entering the filename automatically activates a sequence of DOS commands. As such, batch file commands are components of DOS's primitive programming language.)
   - ECHO Subcommand—displays or supresses the screen display without affecting the execution of batch file commands. Normally, the syntax for each command is displayed on the screen as the command is activated
   - IF Subcommand—allows DOS command to be executed conditionally in a batch file
   - FOR Subcommand—allows sequential execution of the same DOS command in a batch file
   - GOTO Subcommand—allows branching and the use of subroutines in a batch file
3. Disk/File Maintenance Commands
   - CHKDSK—displays a disk status report, providing data on total disk space, files, directories, free disk space, disk capacity, and total memory. It also displays any error messages
   - COMP—compares one specified set of files with another and reports any mismatches; most often used with the COPY command to ensure identical copies
   - COPY—copies files to another area of the disk or to another disk; also used to combine two or more files
   - DISKCOMP—compares the contents of two disks/diskettes; most often used with the DISKCOPY command to ensure identical copies
   - DISKCOPY—copies the contents of one disk to another; also formats the target disk if necessary

- DEL/ERASE—deletes or erases a specified file from the disk
- FORMAT—prepares the disk for DOS files and reports on any defective areas of the disk
- RENAME—changes the name of a specified file

4. Security-Related Commands
   - BACKUP Command—backs up the specified directories/files onto floppy diskettes or other storage media; makes optimal use of disk storage space
   - RESTORE Command—recopies files/directories back onto the fixed disk that have been backed up using the BACKUP command
   - RECOVER Command—recreates files (excluding data contained in corrupted areas of the disk) from a disk containing a corrupted area
   - ERASE Command Confirmation Prompt—prior to erasing specified files the user must respond with a "yes" to a confirmation prompt and press [ENTER]
   - ATTRIB—(DOS 3.X only) permits the user to designate a file as READ-ONLY or READ/WRITE, or display its current status

5. Input/Output-Related Commands
   - GRAPHICS—when using a graphics printer, prints the contents displayed on a color monitor screen
   - PRINT—allows the user to continue to use the computer while printing output
   - FIND—searches for a specified string in a file or series of files
   - MORE—displays data one page at a time followed by a pause and the message—MORE—
   - SORT—sorts data in ascending or descending order

6. Text Editor (EDLIN) Capabilities
   - Insert Lines, Delete Lines, and so on.
   - COPY LINES Command—copies specified lines to another range of line numbers
   - MOVE LINES Command—moves specified lines to another range of line numbers
   - TRANSFER LINES Command—transfers the lines of a specified file into a file that is currently being edited; i.e., it merges the contents of the two files

7. DOS 3.X Commands
   A number of commands and function calls (for file sharing capabilities) were added in the 3.X versions of DOS primarily to support a network environment. Some of these commands are listed below and are discussed throughout this book.
   - FCBS—used for file sharing only, it specifies the maximum number of files that can be opened at the same time by file control blocks. It also specifies the number of files prevented from closing by DOS when a request to open a file exceeds the maximum number of open files
   - JOIN—permits the user to splice together directories

- LASTDRIVE—specifies the maximum number of drives that can be accessed
- SHARE—loads file sharing support (file sharing tables and file locks) into memory
- VDISK—allows the user to assign a portion of RAM as a virtual disk or temporary storage medium

3.

Disks, Disk Drives, and Disk-Related Commands

The standard XT and AT provide the user with a number of different devices and media for the permanent storage of data. The two machines use fixed disks of different capacities. They use floppy disk drives that differ in both capacity and in physical size. And there are some interesting issues concerning the compatibility of data stored with the different floppy disk drives.

This chapter presents an overview of the different disks and disk drives, and the DOS commands that relate to their use.

3.1. Some Technical Information about Disks and Drives

The IBM XT and AT use several different types of floppy disks and disk drives. The XT uses 360KB floppy disks; the AT may have two different types of floppy disk drives, which use 360KB floppy disks or 1.2MB floppy disks, depending on the drive type. The 1.2MB disks are known as *high-capacity* or *high-density* floppy disks. The floppy disk drives on the AT are half the size of the XT's floppy drive; two of the AT floppy drives fit into roughly the same space occupied by one of the XT's floppy drives.

The surfaces of both floppy and hard disks are coated with fine metallic particles that create a magnetic recording surface. Magnetic fields are created by movement of the read-write head across the surface of the disk. Thus, the magnetic polarity of the recording surface allows binary-encoded data (1s and 0s) to be stored. The disk drive or read/write head differs considerably for floppy disk drives, high-capacity drives, and fixed disks. However, in all cases it serves two basic functions:

1. It reads the data stored on the disk by determining the polarity of the magnetic fields at each point on the disk.

2. It stores or writes data on the disk by emitting magnetic pulses that change the polarity of magnetic fields.

Differences between the different types of floppy disks and disk drives are described below.

360KB Floppy Disks and Floppy Disk Drives

Floppy disks are made of polyurethane or Mylar and are covered with iron oxide. The floppy disk is housed in a protective flexible plastic jacket. This jacket contains openings for the disk drive shaft (the centering hole) and for the disk drive read/write head (the head slot). Additionally, a small opening (the index hole window) is located next to the centering hole. When the index hole window lines up with a hole of a similar size in the disk (the timing hole), a beam of light shines through the hole. This light triggers a photosensitive switch that signals to the computer that the disk has completed one revolution.

A small square notch can be found on the right-hand side of most floppy disks. This notch is known as the *Write-Protect notch* because it can be covered with an adhesive tab to prevent disk write-overs and inadvertent erasures. In effect, it restricts the user to Read-Only access.

Once the disk is secured inside the disk drive, it spins inside its protective jacket at approximately 300 rpm. As the disk spins, the read/write head comes into contact with the surface of the disk through the head slot opening in the protective jacket.

The AT's High-Capacity 1.2MB Disks and Drives

High-capacity disks appear identical to 360KB disks. However, these 1.2MB disks are coated with high-coercivity cobalt-modified iron oxide particles. On the AT, the 1.2MB disks fit into disk drives that appear to be identical to the AT's half-height 360KB drives. (The AT's 360KB drive is underneath the 1.2MB floppy drive, and usually is marked by a small asterisk symbol on the lower right-hand corner of the disk drive front panel.)

High-capacity disks spin at 360 rpm, a bit faster than the 300 rpm of floppy disks. The read/write heads are narrower and more sensitive than those of the 360KB drives. Data are also stored more densely on the high-capacity disks; the 360KB disk is formatted with 48 tracks per inch, whereas the high-capacity disk is formatted with 96.

The XT's 10MB Fixed Disk and Disk Drive

The XT fixed disk consists of a set of two 5¼-inch aluminum platters that are coated with iron oxide. Each of the four sides can hold 2½ megabytes of data to constitute a 10-megabyte disk. Both the platters and the recording heads are sealed inside a container that prevents particulate matter from contaminating the highly sensitive recording head mechanisms. This sealed container includes a pressure-equalizing air filter that ensures a contaminant-free environment.

The platters of the fixed disk are fixed on a spindle that rotates at approximately 3600 rpm. This rapidly spinning disk, in combination with the sealed environment, creates air pressure that lifts the recording heads 1.5 microns above the platters' surface. Therefore, with increased rotational speed and recording heads that float above the surface of the disk, the fixed disk drive can store and retrieve data much faster than a floppy disk drive.

Despite the fact that the fixed disk gives the user a much greater recording surface (four sides of the two platters), information on a fixed disk also is recorded even more densely than on a high-capacity floppy disk. Smaller recording heads and greater precision in the movement of the fixed disk drive arm allow significantly more data to be recorded on the disk's surface. For example, data are stored on a 360KB floppy disk with 48 tracks per inch. In comparison, the XT's 10MB fixed disk contains 345 tracks per inch.

The PC-AT 20MB Fixed Disk and Disk Drive

The PC-AT 20MB fixed disk also has two platters or four surfaces of 5MB per side. Unlike the XT, however, the AT 20MB fixed disk has six read/write heads. Only four of these read/write heads are used by current versions of the AT. The rotational speed of the AT's fixed disk (3573 rpm) is not significantly different from the XT's (3600 rpm); however, the AT performs at two times the access speed of the XT's fixed disk.

3.2. The Compatibility of High-Capacity and 360KB Disk Drives

An issue of concern to many AT users is the compatibility of the AT's storage media and disk drives with those of the XT and PC. 360KB disk drives cannot format, read from, or write to high-capacity disks because these disks require a higher write current; only the AT's high-capacity drive may use the high-capacity disks. However, the high-capacity disk drive can be used to format a 360KB disk. This is done by using the "/4" option in the FORMAT command (see the discussion of this command in the next section). This disk then can be used by both the high-capacity drive and the 360KB drives on the XT and PC. Using this technique, data can be transferred from the AT's high-capacity drive to an XT or a PC.

It should be noted that the DOS 3.X manual cautions the user about the "/4" option. It states that 360KB disks formatted with a high-capacity drive may not be *reliably* read or written to with a 360KB drive. However, many users report no problems with this practice when the following procedures are followed:

1. Start with a new disk.
2. Format the disk in the high-capacity drive with the "/4" option.
3. WRITE to that disk only with the high-capacity drive.
4. READ from that disk only with the 360KB drive.

The other option for AT users who require AT/XT/PC upward and downward compatibility is to purchase a 360KB drive for the AT. The Enhanced model AT includes both high-capacity and 360KB disk drives.

Tables 3–1 and 3–2 summarize the formatting and read/write compatibilities between the drive type and media type.

Table 3-1. Formatting Compatibility.

	Storage Media	
Drive Type	**360 KB Floppy Disk**	**High-Capacity Disk**
360KB Floppy Drive	YES Format A:	NO Error message: Invalid media or Track 0 bad—disk unusable Format Failure*
High-Capacity Drive	YES Format A:/4	YES Format A:

*The same error message appears when a high-capacity drive is used to format a 360KB disk without specifying the /4 parameter in the FORMAT command.

Table 3–2. High-Capacity and 360KB Drives: Read/Write Compatibility.

	Storage Media	
Drive Type	**360KB Floppy Disk**	**High-Capacity Disk**
360KB Floppy Drive	YES	NO Error message: Disk error reading drive...
High-Capacity Drive	YES	YES

3.3. DOS System Prompts and Default Drives

When an XT or AT is turned on, or when a system reset is performed, the computer first attempts to load an operating system from the floppy disk drive. IF the DOS program diskette is in the floppy drive and the drive door is closed, the computer loads the DOS operating system from the DOS disk-ette in drive A. The DOS system prompt then appears as:

`A>`

Drive A has become the default drive. This means that DOS will read and write all of its information from the floppy disk drive unless it is told to do otherwise.

As mentioned above, the computer first attempts to load an operating system from the floppy disk drive during a system startup or reset. If there is no disk in drive A, or the drive door is open, the computer then attempts to load the operating system from drive C, the fixed disk. If this is successful, then the DOS system prompt that is displayed is:

`C>`

Drive C is the default drive in this case.

Most of the time, the user will want to have the fixed disk as the default drive. This is because the fixed disk will probably be the location for most of the information stored or retrieved by the computer. However, the default drive may be changed at any time. If the A> prompt is the default, it can be changed to C> by entering this simple command:

`c:`

Drive C is now the default, and the C> prompt is displayed on the screen. Similarly, the C> prompt can be changed back to A> by entering

`a:`

3.4. Formatting Disks

The FORMAT command initializes a disk in the specified drive so that it can be used by DOS. It causes the disk to be analyzed for any defective areas on the disk. It prepares the disk for file storage by setting up a directory and the File Allocation Table. As an option, FORMAT also will copy onto the target disk the DOS files necessary for a system startup. All fixed disk partitions and floppy diskettes must be formatted before they can be used.

How DOS Formats Disks

When a disk is formatted, DOS installs markings that divide the disk's areas into smaller parts. The disk is divided into a series of concentric circles called *tracks*. Each track is divided into smaller sections called *sectors*. A sector can store 512 bytes of information.

The difference between the storage capacities of a fixed disk and a floppy diskette is a function of the number of tracks and sectors. A 360KB floppy diskette formatted with DOS 2.X or 3.X has 40 tracks per side; the XT's fixed disk consists of two platters, and each of the four surfaces has 306 tracks; and each of the AT's four surfaces has 615 tracks. The XT's and the AT's fixed disks have 17 sectors per track; high-capacity diskettes have 15 sectors per track; and floppy diskettes have only 9 sectors per track.

The Syntax of the FORMAT Command

The FORMAT command is written in the following manner:

```
FORMAT [d:][/S][/1][/8][/V][/B][/4]
```

Note: The "/4" option is not available in DOS 2.0 or 2.1 and is a feature unique to DOS 3.0 and 3.1 for formatting 360KB diskettes with a high-capacity drive. With DOS 3.X, the parameter [d:][path] may be placed in front of the command. Since FORMAT is an external command, this allows the user to specify the particular drive and directory in which the command is located. The pathname is separated from the command name by a backslash (\).

The command parameters have the following meanings:

d: This specifies the drive containing the disk to be formatted.

/S When this parameter is included in the command, the following operating system files are copied to the disk or being formatted:
  IBMBIO.COM
  IBMDOS.COM
  COMMAND.COM
 When these files are contained on a disk, a system startup can be performed using that diskette or disk partition. In computer jargon, this makes the partition or diskette "bootable." That is, one is able to "boot" or start the system from the disk.

/1 This is included only when formatting floppy diskettes. It formats the diskette as a single-sided diskette, for use in single-sided disk drives. If it is not included in the command, DOS formats diskettes as dual-sided. Dual-sided diskettes cannot be used in single-sided disk drives.

/8 This formats a floppy diskette with 8 sectors per track instead of the usual 9. It cannot be used when the fixed disk is being formatted.

/V When this parameter is included in the command, DOS prompts the user for a volume label. It is written on the disk and serves no other function except to identify the disk or diskette. It cannot be used with the /8 switch.

/B This formats a diskette with 8 sectors per track, leaving space for the operating system files. It is used to create a diskette onto which any version of DOS (1.0, 1.1, or 2.0) can be placed. It cannot be used in formatting the fixed disk or with the /S and /V parameters.

/4 This formats a 360KB double-sided diskette from the high-capacity drive.

Any data stored on a disk partition or a floppy diskette are destroyed when the disk or diskette is formatted. If the [/S] parameter is used, various messages and statistics are displayed when the formatting is completed. Figure 3–1 shows the screen display generated when a 360 KB drive is used to format a floppy disk using the /V and /S options.

```
C>format a:/s/v
Insert new diskette for drive A:
and strike any key when ready

Formatting...Format complete
System transferred

Volume label (11 characters, ENTER for none)? Figures


   362496 bytes total disk space
    40960 bytes used by system
   321536 bytes available on disk

Format another (Y/N)?n
C>
```

Figure 3–1. Prompts displayed when FORMAT A:/S/V command is entered. /S causes transferral of DOS system files to floppy diskette; /V produces the request for a volume label.

3.5. Other DOS Disk-Related Commands

There are a number of other DOS commands that are used for disk management purposes. Discussed here are the FDISK program, and the SYS (System) and DISKCOPY commands.

The DISKCOPY Command

The entire contents of one floppy diskette can be duplicated on another floppy diskette with this command. The source and target diskettes may be in the same drive or they may be in different drives. If the operation is done on the same drive, DOS prompts the user alternately to insert the source and target diskettes at the appropriate times. The user may find this command more convenient than the COPY command (see Chapter 4), as a way of copying files from one diskette to another.

The command is written in the following format:

```
DISKCOPY [d:] [d:][/1]
```

The parameters in the command have the following meaning:

d: The source and target drives are specified with these parameters. If these parameters are omitted, a single-drive copy operation is performed on the default drive.

/1 When this parameter is included, only the first side of the diskette is copied.

In DOS 3.X, the parameters [d:] and [pathname] may be placed in front of the command to specify the location of the DISKCOPY command.

A single-drive copy would be performed on the diskette in drive A with the following command:

```
diskcopy a: a:
```

The user first is prompted to insert the source diskette (the disk being copied) into drive A. After a few moments, the system then prompts the user to insert the target diskette into drive A. Depending on the amount of memory on the system, the user may be prompted to repeat the operation. When the copy is complete, the system displays the message

```
Copy another (Y/N)?
```

Another copy may be made by entering "Y." If the target diskette has not been formatted, DISKCOPY will format it during the copy operation.

The SYS Command

The SYS (System) command copies the operating system files IBMBIO.COM and IBMDOS.COM from the default drive to the specified drive. It has the following format:

```
SYS d:
```

The [d:] parameter is the drive containing the target disk. To make the target disk bootable (i.e., capable of loading the operating system), the DOS command processor COMMAND.COM file also must be copied onto the target disk, using the COPY command.

In order to use this command, one of the following conditions must exist:

1. The target disk must be completely empty
2. The target disk must have been previously formatted with the command FORMAT d:/S or the command FORMAT d:/B

In other words, a specific location on the target disk must be available for the operating system files. If this is not the case, the following error message is displayed:

`No room for system on destination disk`

This command has a number of useful applications. For example, many application programs such as Lotus 1-2-3 are not sold with DOS contained on the program diskettes. The SYS command allows the user to make such diskettes capable of booting (starting) the system from those diskettes. One must remember to copy the COMMAND.COM file onto the target diskette.

This command also is useful when a user wishes to change the version of DOS that resides on a fixed disk. Rather than reformatting the entire fixed disk, the SYS command could be used instead.

Partitioning a Fixed Disk

When the fixed disk is being used for the first time, it must first be partitioned, and then a DOS partition must be formatted. The set-up routine includes partitioning the fixed disk. This is done by running the FDISK program. DOS allows the user to divide the fixed disk into four separate areas or partitions. In effect, the fixed disk can be divided into four smaller fixed disks. Each of these partitions can contain a different operating system. These four partitions can vary in size; during installation, the user determines the size of each partition by specifying the number of cylinders used by each partition. However, the most common configuration of the fixed disk is a single partition (i.e., the entire fixed disk is used by one partition, the DOS partition).

For most users, the only time this command is used is when the system is set up. However, there are a few occasions in which this command is used. For example, if the user wishes to add another, non-DOS operating system to the fixed disk, it would be necessary to back up data on the fixed disk, run the FDISK program to repartition the fixed disk, and then restore the data to the DOS partition. The FDISK program also would be used if another hard disk were added to a system.

The program is contained on the main DOS diskette. With this diskette in the A drive, it is executed by simply entering the command

`a:fdisk`

When this command is entered, DOS displays the information shown in Figure 3–2 on the screen. Note that the default choice is to create a DOS partition (1). If the system contains a second hard disk drive, a fifth choice on the menu is displayed:

5. Select Next Fixed Drive

The first menu choice is used to create a DOS partition. If the fixed disk is to contain more than one operating system, the other, non-DOS partitions are created with the operating systems that are to occupy them.

Option 2 on the FDISK menu allows the user to designate an active partition. That is, the active partition is the partition in which the computer looks for the operating system when it is turned on or when a system restart is performed. A DOS partition is the active partition by default unless the user specifies a different one.

To display information on how the fixed disk has been partitioned, option 4 from the FDISK Options menu is selected. The screen display generated by this command is shown in Figure 3–3. Under the headings *Partition*, *Status*, *Type*, and so on, appear one to four lines, depending on the number of partitions on the fixed disk. In Figure 3–3, there is only one line because the fixed disk generating the screen display for the figure had only one partition.

```
IBM Personal Computer
Fixed Disk Setup Program Version 1.00
(C)Copyright IBM Corp. 1983

FDISK Options


Choose one of the following:

        1.   Create DOS Partition
        2.   Change Active Partition
        3.   Delete DOS Partition
        4.   Display Partition Data


Enter choice: [1]




Press Esc to return to DOS
```

Figure 3–2. Menu generated by FDISK command.

```
IBM Personal Computer
Fixed Disk Setup Program Version 1.00
(C)Copyright IBM Corp. 1983

Display Partition Information


Partition Status    Type   Start  End Size
    1         A     DOS        0  304  305



Total disk space is  305 cylinders.




Press Esc to return to FDISK Options [  ]
```

Figure 3–3. Screen generated by FDISK command option 4.

3.6. A Summary of Information on Disks, Drives, and Related Commands

1. Floppy disks can be 360KB or 1.2MB (high-capacity); the standard XT comes with a 10MB fixed disk and the enhanced AT comes with one 20MB fixed disk.
2. The magnetic polarity of the disk recording surface allows binary-encoded data (1s and 0s) to be stored. Disk drive read/write heads read data stored on the disk by determining the polarity of the magnetic fields at each point on the disk. Read/write heads store data on the disk by emitting magnetic pulses that change the polarity of magnetic fields.
3. The fixed disk drive can store and retrieve data much faster than a floppy disk drive.
4. The AT's fixed disk performs at two times the access speed of the XT's fixed disk.
5. 360KB drives cannot format, read from, or write to high-capacity disks. However, high-capacity disk drives can be used to format a 360KB disk. This permits data transfer from an AT high-capacity drive to an XT drive.
6. When formatting a 360KB disk in a high-capacity drive, it is a good idea to: use a fresh disk; format the disk with the "/4" option; WRITE

on the disk only with the high-capacity drive; and READ the disk only with a 360KB drive.

7. The default drive on the XT or AT is C.

8. The FORMAT command prepares a disk to be used by DOS. It analyzes any defective areas on the disk and prepares the disk for file storage by establishing a directory and the File Allocation Table.

9. The FORMAT command divides the disk into tracks. Each track is divided into sectors. Each sector can store 512 characters.

10. FORMAT is an external DOS command.

11. Data stored on a disk are destroyed when the disk is formatted.

12. The DISKCOPY command copies the contents of one diskette to another. This process also formats the target disk.

13. The SYS command copies the DOS files IBMBIO.COM and IBMDOS.COM to a target disk. This command is useful when the user wishes to change the version of DOS that resides on the fixed disk without reformatting the entire fixed disk.

14. During setup, a fixed disk must be partitioned; a DOS partition must then be formatted. This is done with the FDISK command. The FDISK command also is used when one wishes to add another non-DOS operating system and if another hard disk is added to the system.

4.

Hierarchical Directories

Information stored on the fixed disk of the XT and AT can be organized by function and type. This is one of the most important features of DOS, since thousands of files may be placed on the fixed disk. The storage capacity of a 20-megabyte fixed disk is approximately 56 times greater than that of a single 360K floppy diskette and 17 times that of a high-capacity diskette. With a large amount of information stored on the fixed disk, locating a specific file could be a slow process. However, with DOS, quick access of information on the fixed disk can be achieved through the use of *Hierarchical Directories*.

The directory is the area of a disk that contains information about what is stored on the disk. All formatted disks have at least one directory. DOS 2.X. and 3.X both allow the use of multiple directories on floppy diskettes, high-capacity diskettes, and fixed disks. These directories are structured in a user-designed hierarchy. An understanding of hierarchical directories is essential for the efficient management of the XT and AT. This chapter describes the various components of hierarchical directories, and how they are created, used, and managed.

4.1. Directories and Subdirectories

The first task in designing a hierarchical directory system is deciding how the directory system is to be structured. DOS gives the user a great deal of flexibility in setting up a hierarchical directory. When a disk is formatted, DOS starts the basic organization of the directory system by creating one main directory. The structure of the directory system after this point is determined by the user. This section describes the structure of hierarchical directories, and the DOS commands involved in the creation, use, and display of these directories.

The Structure of Hierarchical Directories

The manner in which hierarchical directories are organized is similar to the structure of a corporate organizational chart. The starting point for all hierarchical directories is the *Root Directory*. In the organizational chart analogy, the root directory would be the top of the chart or, more specifically, the corporate office.

All formatted disks contain a root directory in DOS 2.X and 3.X. The root directory may contain programs, data files, or the names of other directories (subdirectories). However, many individuals prefer to limit the root directory to system or program files. Each directory within the root directory may contain its own set of programs, data files, or directories (sub-subdirectories). This type of organization is often referred to as a *Tree-structured directory*. The branching of directories into subdirectories may be extended out as far as necessary.

Hierarchical directories may be structured in any manner that is convenient for the user. To demonstrate how a directory might be organized, consider the following example. The fixed disk on a PC-AT is used to store DOS files, a word processing program, and a spreadsheet program. The root directory contains the DOS files and a separate directory for the word processing program. The word processing directory, called TEXT, contains the files that constitute the word processing program, as well as two subdirectories of its own; these subdirectories contain the word processing data files. One of these subdirectories is called LETTERS and the other is called REPORTS. The LETTERS subdirectory contains a subdirectory of its own for a special category of letters; it is called DUNNING. The structure of the directory up to this point is shown in Figure 4–1. Notice that it is not necessary for a directory to contain any files. The DUNNING directory is empty.

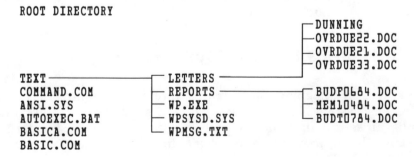

Figure 4–1. Diagram of a hierarchical directory system, showing the root directory and one subdirectory.

The root directory of this hypothetical directory system also contains a separate directory for the spreadsheet program, called SHEET. In the SHEET directory are the files that make up the spreadsheet program and a subdirectory for the program's data files; the subdirectory is called BUDGETS. More subdirectories might be added to the SHEET directory as needed. Another subdirectory in the SHEET directory, called DJDATA, could be available for files downloaded from a mainframe. Figure 4–2 shows how this directory system now looks with the addition of the SHEET directory.

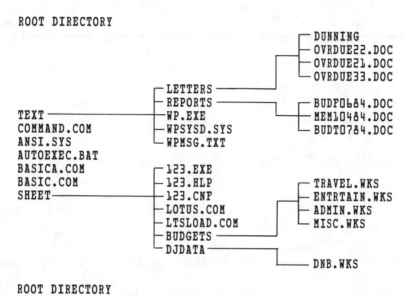

ROOT DIRECTORY

Figure 4–2. Expanded version of the directory system shown in Figure 4–1, showing the root directory, two subdirectories, and their subdirectories.

Tree-structured directories are useful for a number of reasons. One advantage is that related groups of files may be placed together in the same directory. This is particularly useful when several different individuals are using the same XT or AT and storing information on the fixed disk. Each person might store his or her files in a specific directory or set of directories.

Another advantage of tree-structured directories is related to the capacity of the root directory relative to subdirectories. The size of the root directory is fixed and can only hold a limited number of entries, even if the hard disk is not filled to capacity. In contrast, subdirectories within a tree-structured hierarchy are actually files, and can therefore contain an unlimited number of entries.

Tree-structured directories also allow DOS to quickly locate a specified file. This is because DOS sees only the files contained in the specified directory when it is searching for a file. The system is able to do this by using a pathname that precedes the filename. A pathname specifies each directory through which DOS must move in order to access the specific file. Each directory in the pathname is separated by the backslash symbol (\). For example, in Figure 4–2, the pathname for the file OVRDUE22.DOC (starting from the root directory) would be

`C:\TEXT\LETTERS\OVRDUE22.DOC`

Note that a backslash also separates the directory name from the filename.

A tree-structured directory can contain as many subdirectory levels as necessary. There is no limitation on the number of subdirectories that may be created, except that sufficient disk space must be available. However, DOS cannot accept pathnames that exceed 63 characters, including the backslash characters.

In the directory of Figure 4–2, there are three directory levels. Many more could be added. Each directory may contain numerous files and subdirectories. The number of files that may be placed in a directory is limited only by the amount of space available on the disk or in the DOS partition.

Creating Directories and Subdirectories

Directories and subdirectories are created with two DOS commands. A root directory is created automatically whenever a disk or DOS partition is formatted. This is done with the command FORMAT. (The procedure for formatting disks is discussed in detail in Chapter 3.) All other directories are created with the command MKDIR (Make Directory). This command may be abbreviated to MD.

The MKDIR command has the following format:

`MKDIR [d:][path][dirname]`

The parameters in this command have the following meaning:

d: This specifies the disk drive that is to contain the new directory.

path This is a series of directory names that leads DOS from the current or root directory through the directory hierarchy to the level at which the new directory is to be placed. A backslash separates each directory name in a path.

dirname This is the name of the new directory. The directory name is separated from the path by a backslash.

The drive and path specifications are optional. When they are not specified in the command, the new directory is placed in the current directory of the default drive.

The term *Current Directory* requires some further explanation. The current, or active, directory is the location in the hierarchy from which DOS is reading files at a point in time. A new directory that is created with the MKDIR command is placed as a subdirectory of the current directory unless a path is specified. DOS always begins with the root directory as the current directory when the system is booted. The current directory may be changed with the command CHDIR (Change Directory). This command is discussed in more detail later in this chapter.

Using the MKDIR Command

The MKDIR command is used to create new directories at all levels of the directory hierarchy. This can be demonstrated by observing how subdirectories are created for the directory system shown in Figure 4–2.

Assume that the current directory is the root directory. The root directory contains two subdirectories (TEXT and SHEET). These were created with the following commands (MD can also be used as an abbreviated command for Make Directory):

`MKDIR TEXT`

`MKDIR SHEET`

Either upper- or lower-case letters are acceptable. Also, the MKDIR command may be abbreviated to MD. Since no drive is specified in the command, the new directories are placed in the root directory of the default drive. If it is necessary to include the drive parameter when creating a new directory, the commands are written as:

`MD A:TEXT`

`MD A:SHEET`

When the current directory is not the root directory, the commands are written as:

`MD \TEXT`

`MD \SHEET`

A pathname parameter that begins with a backslash indicates that the starting point in the path is the root directory.

To add the REPORTS and LETTERS subdirectories to the newly-created TEXT directory, either the current directory must be changed so that TEXT is the current directory (using the CHDIR command described below), or a path must be specified in the MD command. If the current directory is still the root directory, then the commands would be written as:

```
MD TEXT\LETTERS
```

```
MD TEXT\REPORTS
```

If the current directory is neither the root directory nor the TEXT directory, the path must begin with the root directory:

```
MD \TEXT\LETTERS
```

```
MD \TEXT\REPORTS
```

Notice that the backslash is used to separate the directory names in a path, in addition to specifying the root directory as the beginning of the path. To add the DUNNING subdirectory to the LETTERS directory, the command might be written as:

```
MD \TEXT\LETTERS\DUNNING
```

There often are a number of ways to specify a path. However, it is good practice to start a path at the root directory level: That way, one can be certain that the new directory is placed in the correct location in the hierarchy.

Naming Directories

There are a few rules that must be followed in naming directories. Generally, they are similar to the rules governing filenames. The rules are as follows:

1. A directory name may contain 1 to 8 characters. An optional extension may be added to the name, and may be 1 to 3 characters in length. The extension is separated from the directory name by a period.
2. The characters that may be used in a directory name include all upper- and lower-case letters, the numbers 0 to 9, and the following special symbols:

    > @ # $ & ( ) — _ « » ’ ~

    DOS automatically converts all lower-case letters to upper case.
3. Spaces, commas, and all other symbols other than those listed above are not allowed.
4. Certain device names that are used by DOS (e.g., CON, AUX, PRN, etc.) are reserved words. These words cannot be used as directory names.

These are examples of valid directory names:

`WORDPROC.WST`

`WORDPROC.MM`

`4TH_QRTR`

`123`

These are examples of invalid directory names:

SPREADSHEET   (too many characters)

4TH QRTR   (contains a space)

DOS+QUAD   (illegal character)

One always must be careful to use only the valid special characters in directory names. Certain invalid special characters, such as the * symbol, can have very unpredictable results. Also, it is a good practice to use directory names that are meaningful and easily remembered.

Displaying the Hierarchy

DOS has several commands that can be used to display the directory hierarchy. All filenames and directories, or only the contents of a specific directory, may be displayed. The screen display also may be redirected to the printer. This can be particularly useful when the contents of a directory are too extensive to be viewed on a single screen.

The DIR Command

The DOS command DIR (Directory) will display the contents of a directory. The DIR command has the following format:

`DIR [d:][path][filename][/P][/S]`

The parameters in this command have the following meaning:

d: This specifies the disk drive containing the directory that is to be displayed.

path   This is a series of directory names that leads DOS from the current or root directory through the directory hierarchy to the directory to be displayed. A backslash separates each directory name in a path.

filename   A specific filename or a category of files (if wild cards are used) is displayed when this parameter is used.

/P   This causes the display to pause after the screen is full.

/W   Filenames are shown in a wide display, with five filenames on each line.

All of the above parameters are optional. If no drive is specified, then the default drive is assumed. If no path or filename is given, then DOS will display the contents of the current directory.

The directory system of Figure 4–2 can be used to demonstrate how this command may be used. Assume that drive C on a PC-AT contains this directory system. Entering the DIR command without any parameters produces the following information when in the root directory of C:\ :

```
Volume in drive C has no label

Directory of  C:\


COMMAND  COM    17664    4-20-84   12:26a

AUTOEXEC BAT       36    4-20-84   12:31a

ANSI     SYS       45    4-20-84   12:26p

BASICA   COM       45    4-20-84   12:26p

BASIC    COM       45    4-20-84   12:26p

TEXT          <DIR>      4-21-84   12:45a

SHEET         <DIR>      4-21-84   12:47a

7 File(s)    9275648 bytes free
```

The first line of this display indicates that the disk was not given a volume name at the time it was formatted. This is of no consequence. The second line indicates that this is a display of the root directory in drive C. The root directory is always denoted by a backslash.

When the contents of a directory are displayed with the the DIR command, subdirectories are considered as files. Thus, the above information specifies that there are seven files in this directory, although, in actuality, there are only five files and two subdirectories. Notice that subdirectories are identified by the <DIR> marking.

DOS displays some slightly different information when the DIR command is issued outside of the root directory. For example, suppose the current directory in Figure 4–2 is the SHEET directory. The DIR command, issued without any of its parameters, would produce the following information:

```
Volume in drive C has no label
Directory of  C:\SHEET


.              <DIR>      4-21-84   12:45a

..             <DIR>      4-21-84   12:47a

123     EXE     89856   5-01-84    2:03p

123     HLP    113416   5-01-84    2:03p

123     CNF       256   5-01-84    2:03p

LOTUS   COM       481   5-01-84    2:03p

LTSLOAD COM     10144   5-01-84    2:03p

BUDGETS        <DIR>      5-01-84    2:47p

DJDATA         <DIR>      5-01-84    2:52p

9 File(s)    8875648 bytes free
```

The second line shows that this is a display of the contents of the SHEET directory. More unusual, however, are the entries shown for the first two files: The first of these entries shows a period in place of a filename, and the second shows two periods in place of a filename. Both are listed as directories. The single-period entry denotes the directory being listed. The double-period entry denotes the parent directory of the directory being listed. The *Parent Directory* is the higher-level directory that contains the subdirectory. In the case of the example above, the parent of SHEET is the root directory. The TREE command (discussed later) is used to show the parent relationship of various subdirectories.

The double-period notation can be used to display the contents of a subdirectory's parent directory. This can be accomplished by writing the DIR command as:

```
DIR ..
```

Any DIR command parameters may be used with this notation.

Disk drive and pathnames may be specified in the DIR command. This means that the contents of a directory may be displayed without changing the default drive or the current directory. For example, suppose the default drive is the fixed disk drive (drive C). The following command displays the contents of the root directory for a disk in drive A:

```
DIR A:\
```

In the next example, suppose the default drive is drive A. The following command displays the contents of a subdirectory contained in a fixed disk's root directory:

```
DIR C:\SHEET
```

Taking this one step further, the following command displays the contents of a subdirectory in the SHEET directory:

```
DIR C:\SHEET\BUDGETS
```

The DIR command has two additional parameters that are useful when the contents of a directory exceed the size of the screen. The /P parameter causes the listing of a directory's contents to pause when the screen is full. Pressing any key resumes the directory listing. The /W parameter produces a wide display of a directory's contents. Only the names of subdirectories and files are shown, and each line contains five names. The file size, the <DIR> symbols, and the date and time specifications are not listed.

When all the DIR parmeters are included in the command, they should appear in the following order:

```
DIR C:\SHEET\BUDGETS\*.WKS/P/W
```

Notice that the filename parameter uses the global or wild-card character to display the names of all the filenames with a .WKS filename extension. Also, the pause and wide display parameters use the slash character as separators, not the backslash. A DIR command may include either or both the /P and /W parameters, and they may be used with or without the drive, path, and filename specifications. For example, the command

```
DIR /W
```

produces a wide display of the current directory on the default drive. Figures 4–3 and 4–4 show the types of screen output generated by the pause and wide display parameters.

```
dir \software/p

Volume in drive C is XTMGMT
Directory of C:\software

.                 <DIR>        1-01-80     1:56a
..                <DIR>        1-01-80     1:56a
123      EXE      89856        1-01-80
123      HLP     113416        6-07-83     1:23a
123      CNF        256        4-21-84    12:01a
LOTUS    COM        481        6-07-83     1:23a
LOTUS    DLB      40889        6-07-83     1:23a
GRAPH    EXE      62080        6-07-83     1:23a
GRAPH    HLP      20747        6-07-83     1:23a
GRAPH    CNF        384       10-27-83     7:36p
LTSLOAD  COM      10144        6-07-83     1:23a
TD       DRV       5294        6-07-83     1:23a
KB       DRV        352        6-07-83     1:23a
PR       DRV        329        6-07-83     1:23a
IBMOHERC DRV       5293        6-07-83     1:23a
IBMOMONO DRV        745        6-07-83     1:23a
IBMOB&W  DRV       5294        6-07-83     1:23a
IBMOCOLO DRV       5294        6-07-83     1:23a
IBM1HERC DRV       2080        6-07-83     1:23a
IBM1G1   DRV       2139        6-07-83     1:23a
IBM1G2   DRV       2139        6-07-83     1:23a
IBM2KB   DRV        352        6-07-83     1:23a
IBM3PR   DRV        329        6-07-83     1:23a
Strike a key when ready . . .
```

Figure 4–3. Example of screen output generated by DIR command when /P switch is used. /P causes display to pause after every 23 lines of output.

```
C>dir\software/w
 Volume in drive C is XTMGMT
 Directory of C:\software

.                  ..                  123      EXE    123      HLP    123      CNF
LOTUS    COM    LOTUS    DLB    GRAPH    EXE    GRAPH    HLP    GRAPH    CNF
LTSLOAD  COM    TD       DRV    KB       DRV    PR       DRV    IBMOHERC DRV
IBMOMONO DRV    IBMOB&W  DRV    IBMOCOLO DRV    IBM1HERC DRV    IBM1G1   DRV
IBM1G2   DRV    IBM2KB   DRV    IBM3PR   DRV    CPQOTD   DRV    GD       DRV
        25 File(s)   7622656 bytes free

C>
```

Figure 4–4. Example of screen output generated by DIR command when /W switch is used. /W produces a wide display of a directory's filenames, with five filenames per line.

The TREE command

The TREE command (Display Directory) allows the user to view the structure of the disk's entire directory system. The difference between this command and the DIR command is that the latter permits the display of only one directory at a time. The TREE command has the following format:

TREE [d:][/F]

> **d:** This specifies the disk drive containing the directory system to be displayed.
> **/F** When this parameter is included, the TREE command displays the names of files contained in each directory.

Note: With DOS 3.X, the parameter [d:][path] may be placed in front of the command. Since TREE is an external command, this allows the user to specify the particular drive and directory in which the command file is located. The pathname is separated from the command by a backslash (\).

Both the drive and the /F parameters are optional. If the drive parameter is not specified, the TREE command displays the directories on the default drive. TREE displays only directory names and directory paths unless the /F parameter is used. Figure 4–5 shows part of the output generated for a TREE command using the drive and /F parameters for the hierarchical directory of Figure 4–2. Notice that the paths, subdirectories, and files are clearly specified. The TREE command can be a particularly effective method of keeping track of what is contained in an extensive directory system.

```
tree /f

DIRECTORY PATH LISTING FOR VOLUME ??????????

Path: \TEXT

Sub-directories:   LETTERS
                   REPORTS

Files:             WP        .EXE
                   WPSYSD    .SYS
                   WPMSG     .TXT


Path: \TEXT\LETTERS

Sub-directories:   DUNNING

Files:             OVRDUE22.DOC
                   OVRDUE21.DOC
                   OVRDUE  .DOC


Path: \TEXT\LETTERS\DUNNING

Sub-directories:   None

Files:             None


Path: \TEXT\REPORTS

Sub-directories:   None

Files:             BUDF0684.DOC
                   MEM10484.DOC
                   BUDT0784.DOC
```

Figure 4–5. Example of screen output generated by TREE command when /F switch is used. /F causes TREE to list filenames in the directories. ??? symbols following volume name indicate that disk has no label.

Redirecting the Output of the DIR and TREE Commands

Sometimes a directory system is so extensive that it is useful to have a hard copy of its contents. The output of the DIR and TREE commands may be redirected to the printer. That is, the information can be printed instead of being displayed on the screen. This is done by writing the commands in the following way:

```
DIR>PRN
```

PRN is a reserved device name used by DOS to specify the printer. The symbol > is used to redirect the output of a DOS command. All other parameters may be included. For example, the data in Figure 4–5 were printed with the command

```
TREE C:/F>PRN
```

Redirecting the output of the TREE command to the printer is useful because the TREE command's display often will not fit on a single screen.

4.2. Moving through the Directory Hierarchy

There are a number of ways to direct DOS through the directory hierarchy. When using commands such as DIR and MKDIR, pathnames can be used to to guide DOS to the appropriate level in a directory system.

Using Pathnames

In any command that uses the path parameter, DOS may be directed to a specific level in the directory hierarchy. The ERASE command is one such command. To demonstrate how a pathname might be used with this command, consider again the directory system of Figure 4–2. Suppose the current directory is the root directory, and a user wished to erase the TRAVEL.WKS file in the BUDGET directory. This could be accomplished with the following command (see Figure 4–6):

```
ERASE \SHEET\BUDGETS\TRAVEL.WKS
```

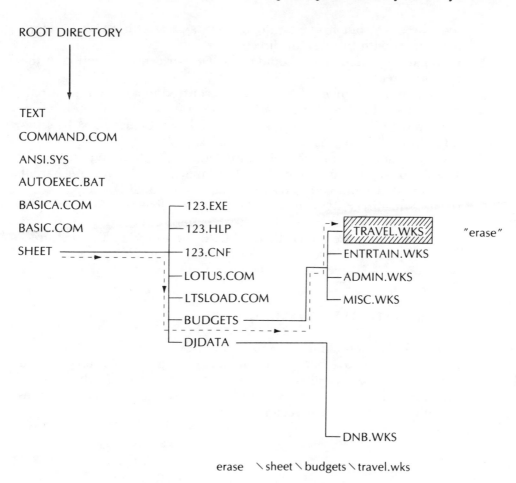

erase \ sheet \ budgets \ travel.wks

Figure 4–6. The path travelled by DOS to erase the TRAVEL.WKS file. Path begins at root directory level.

Note that the first backslash in the pathname denotes the root directory. The subsequent backslash characters separate the directory names and filenames from one another. Below are listed a few points that should be remembered in using pathnames.

Some Rules and Suggestions for Using Pathnames

1. The root directory is always designated by a backslash at the beginning of a pathname. It is not necessary to start a pathname with the

root directory, but if it is omitted, DOS assumes that the directory path starts with the current directory.

2. If no path is specified in a command, DOS performs the action in the current directory.

3. The maximum number of characters permitted in a pathname is 63.

4. When more than one directory is specified in a path, each directory name must be separated by a backslash. Filenames also must be separated from directory names by a backslash.

5. Global filename characters (wild cards) are not allowed in pathnames.

6. The double-period notation that DOS uses to designate the parent directory of a subdirectory may be used as a pathname. This makes it possible to direct DOS up one level in the directory. For example, suppose the current directory for the hierarchy of Figure 4–2 is REPORTS. To erase the OVERDUE.DOC file in the LETTERS directory, the path could ascend to the parent directory level of REPORTS (which is TEXT), and then move down the hierarchy to the specified file (See Figure 4–7):

`ERASE ..\LETTERS\OVRDUE33.DOC`

The double-period notation denotes the TEXT directory.

7. Since the specified action is performed in the current directory when a pathname is not specified, it is often easier to change the current directory than it is to specify a path. This is done with the DOS command CHDIR (Change Directory).

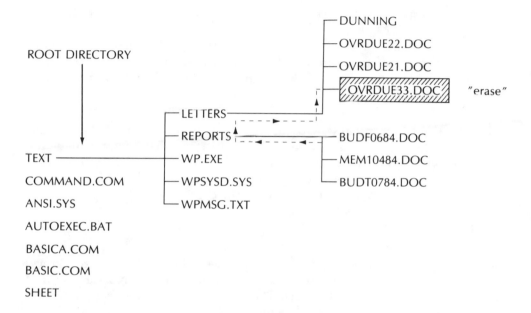

erase . . \ letters \ ovrdue33.doc

Figure 4–7. The path travelled by DOS when the double-dot (parent directory) notation is used. This is the only time a path can move up a level in the hierarchy without starting at the root directory. If the current directory is REPORTS, DOS first moves up a level to the TEXT directory and then moves back down to the LETTERS directory.

Using the CHDIR Command

Many times it is easier to change the current directory rather than use pathnames in DOS commands. This is most logical when the same directory is frequently accessed for data files or commands. The current directory may be changed with the CHDIR (Change Directory) command. This command may be abbreviated to CD.

The CHDIR command has the following format:

```
CHDIR [d:][path]
```

The parameters in this command have the following meaning:

d: This specifies the disk drive of the directory to be the current directory.

path This is a series of directory names that leads DOS from the current or root directory through the hierarchy to a newly designated current directory. A backslash separates each directory name in a path.

Entering the CD command with no parameters will display the current directory. The drive specification is optional. If no drive is specified, the default drive is assumed. In the directory system of Figure 4–2, suppose that the current directory is the root directory. The current directory could be changed to the BUDGETS directory with the command

```
CD SHEET\BUDGETS
```

Note that the path does not start with a backslash (the root directory) because the current directory is already the root directory. Notice also that CHDIR can be abbreviated to CD. The current directory can be changed back to the root directory with the command

```
CD  \
```

Using the PATH Command

The PATH command also directs DOS through specific directories whenever the current directory does not contain the requested batch file or command. DOS first searches the current directory for the specified command or batch file. If it is not found, DOS then looks in certain other directories. These "alternate" directories are specified by the PATH command. The PATH command is particularly useful with hierarchical directories because DOS does not permit the execution of a program or batch file that is not in the current directory. The directory system of Figure 4–8 is used to demonstrate how this command works.

The root directory contains a subdirectory called UTILITY. This directory contains a number of DOS program files as well as the IBM Advanced Basic program. Unless the PATH command is used, the current directory must be UTILITY in order to load the BASICA program. For example, if the command BASICA is entered, and the current directory is the root directory, the following error message is displayed:

```
Bad command or file name
```

The PATH command instructs DOS to search through a specified directory or directories for commands and/or batch files not found in the current directory. More than one path may be specified, and the drive may be specified as well.

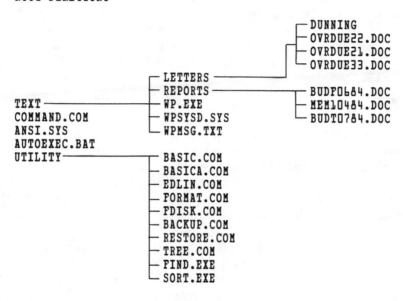

```
ROOT DIRECTORY
```

Figure 4–8. Diagram of a directory system with a subdirectory for DOS programs.

The PATH command has the following format:

```
PATH [d:]path1;[d:]path2;[d:]path3;...
```

d:	This specifies the disk drive of the directory that is to be searched for commands or batch files.
path1; path2; path3;	These are pathnames that direct DOS to the directories in the hierarchy where commands or batch files may be found. When more than one is specified, each is separated by a semicolon.

The drive specification is an optional parameter. For the directory of Figure 4–8, PATH permits activation of the BASICA program from any directory or drive specification:

`PATH C:\UTILITY`

Note that the path starts at the root directory. If more than one directory path is specified, the command might have the following format:

`PATH C:\;C:\UTILITY`

After the above command has been entered, when subsequent commands are entered, DOS first searches the current directory for a specified command or batch file. If the command is not found in the current directory, it then searches the root directory of the drive C disk. If it is still not found, DOS searches the UTILITY directory in drive C.

Rules and Suggestions in Using the PATH Command

1. If no disk drive is specified for a path, the current drive is used.
2. More than one directory path may be specified in the PATH command; each must be separated by a semicolon.
3. It is a good idea to always start paths from the root directory. If the root directory is not the starting point in a path, DOS assumes that the path begins with the current directory. This may result in an invalid path.
4. Any path that contains invalid information (such as a bad drive name or a nonexistent directory) will be ignored.
5. Only program command files and batch files are affected by the PATH command (i.e., files with filename extensions of .EXE, .COM, or .BAT).
6. The PATH command can be most useful when it is included in an AUTOEXEC.BAT file. This file type is automatically executed when a system or program is booted. For example, the DOS 3.0 disk contains an AUTOEXEC.BAT file that automatically issues the DATE and TIME commands. The same file also might contain a PATH command. Then, DOS will search the specified directories for any subsequent command or batch file not found in the current directory during a DOS session. (The chapter on batch files discusses the subject of creating and modifying AUTOEXEC.BAT files in detail.)
7. Directory paths specified by the PATH command are in effect only in the DOS environment.
8. The PATH command without parameters displays the current path.

4.3. Management and Organization of a Directory Hierarchy

A directory system is only as effective as its organization is efficient. A good hierarchical directory should be no more complex than is necessary. Subdirectories should be organized according to the type of files that they will contain. It is best to keep directory names short and simple.

Many applications programs allow the user to store and access data files in multiple subdirectories from within the specific program. If users of such programs are likely to generate hundreds of data files, it is a good idea to create several subdirectories for the program's files. In a program such as 1-2-3, it takes much less time to retrieve a file when the user is not forced to search through a list of all 1-2-3 data files stored on the fixed disk.

Eliminating Files from a Hierarchical Directory

Although the fixed disk can store a great deal of information, it has a finite capacity. Eventually, it will become necessary to eliminate unnecessary files. The ERASE and DEL (Delete) commands are used for ongoing maintenance of this type. These two commands have identical functions and format:

ERASE [d:][path][filename]

DEL [d:][path][filename]

The parameters in these commands have the following meaning:

d: This specifies the disk drive containing the file that is to be erased.

path   This leads DOS through the hierarchy to the directory containing the file that is to be erased.

filename The file that is to be eliminated is specified by this parameter. If a path is specified, a backslash separates the pathname from the filename.

If no drive or path is specified, the file is deleted from the current directory of the default drive. Files that have been marked READ-ONLY cannot be erased. (Files are marked READ-ONLY with the ATTRIB command; see Chapter 10 for a discussion of this command.)

More than one file may be erased at a time when the global filename characters (wild cards) are used. These characters are the * and ? symbols. They are used to designate files in a more generalized, less exacting manner. The * symbol permits substitution of up to eight characters for the symbol. Below are examples of how it might be used:

B*.*   Specifies all files that begin with the letter "B." The filenames BUDGET.WKS, BILLS.WKS, and BILLS.DOC would be included.

*.DOC   Specifies all files that have a filename extension of .DOC. The filenames REPORT.DOC, MEMO.DOC, and MEMO2.DOC would be included.

.   Specifies all files in a directory.

The ? symbol allows substitution of a single character for the symbol in a filename. Below are some examples of how it might be used:

QUARTER?.WKS   Any one character may be placed in the filename for the ? symbol. QUARTER1.WKS, QUARTER2.WKS, and QUARTER.WKS would be included in this specification.

QRTR?BUD.DOC   QRTR1BUD.DOC and QRTR2BUD.DOC would be specified by this filename.

Some Suggestions in Using the ERASE and DEL Commands

1. Use the *.* filename designation with caution. Because the *.* filename specification designates all files in a directory, DOS displays the following warning prompt when *.* is used with ERASE or DEL:

    ```
    Are you sure (Y/N)?
    ```

    Entering an "N" cancels the command. A "Y" answer must be followed by an ENTER.

2. The DIR command should be issued before using ERASE or DEL commands that contain wild card characters. The same wild card can be used to display the files that will be affected by the erasure. Thus, the user will be certain that only the intended files are deleted. For example, the command

    ```
    DIR *.WKS
    ```

    displays all files in the current directory with filename extensions of .WKS.

3. The current directory and default drive are assumed. It is recommended that the commands ERASE and DEL be used only within the current directory. However, just in case, one should always specify a path when using the *.* designation in the ERASE and DEL commands. This helps prevent the inadvertent erasure of data.

4. It is possible to recover erased files if no new information is placed on the disk after the ERASE or DEL commands have been issued. This is because these commands do not actually wipe out areas of the disk, but rather specify that the space occupied by the "erased" files is now available for data storage; if no new information is added to the disk,

the files remain intact. To recover these files, a special utility program such as UNERASE in the Norton Utilities must be used. The DOS command RECOVER cannot be used for this purpose.

Eliminating Directories from a Hierarchical Directory

Occasionally, it is necessary to eliminate an entire directory from a directory system. The DOS command RMDIR (Remove Directory) is used for this purpose. It may be abbreviated to RD. This command has the format:

```
RMDIR [d:][path]
```

The parameters in this command have the following meaning:

d: This is the drive specification.
path This specifies a directory path, with each directory separated by a backslash. The last name in the path is the directory that is to be deleted.

There are a few rules that must be followed when the RD command is used:

1. The root directory and the current directory cannot be deleted.
2. The directory that is to be deleted must be empty, except for the "." and ".." listings. So use the command ERASE *.* first. When a DIR command is used to display the contents of an empty directory, only two files will be listed: the parent directory (..) and the current directory (.).
3. The name of the directory to be deleted must be specified in the command. If a path is specified, the directory to be deleted must be the last name in the path.
4. If the drive is not specified, the current drive is assumed.

Moving Files from Directory to Directory

Sometimes it is necessary to move a file to another directory. This can be accomplished with the COPY command. This command has many options and parameters. When copying files from one directory to another, the command's parameters first must describe the source file, and then the target file. The *source file* is the file being copied; the *target file* is the duplicate.
   The COPY command has the following format:

```
COPY [/A][/B][d:][path][filename][/A][/B]  [d:][path][filename][/A][/B][/V]
```

The source file parameters in the above command are defined up to and including the first filename parameter; the parameters for the target file are all those thereafter. A space separates the source and target parameters. Although there are many parameters, only a few of these are required when a file is being copied to another directory. The parameters in this command have the following meaning:

/A   If used with the source file, it specifies that the file is copied as an ASCII (text) file. In the target file, it causes an end-of-file character to be added at the end of the file.

/B   If used with the source file, the entire file is copied, based on its directory file size. If used with the target file, no end-of-file character is added to the file.

d: This specifies the drive location for both the source and target files.

path   The path parameter guides DOS to the appropriate level in the directory system for the source and target files.

filename In the source file, this is the file that is to be copied; in the target file, this specifies the duplicate.

/V   This parameter tells DOS to verify that the copy has been recorded correctly.

If no drives are specified when copying files, then the default drive is assumed. Although errors in recording data are rare, the /V parameter can be used to ensure that critical data have been duplicated correctly.

The only parameters required to copy files from one directory to another are the path and filename parameters. DOS will not copy a file with the same filename into a different directory without these. For example, consider again the directory of Figure 4–2. Suppose a user wishes to copy the OVERDUE.DOC file into the REPORTS directory. If the root directory is the current directory, the command would be:

```
COPY TEXT\LETTERS\OVERDUE.DOC TEXT\REPORTS\OVERDUE.DOC
```

When the target file uses the source filename, the filename parameter may be omitted for the target file. Thus in the above command, the second reference to "OVERDUE.DOC" could have been eliminated. When the path parameter is also omitted in the target file, the file is copied under the same name into the current directory. Note the space between the source and target parameters. If the above command is entered as

```
COPY TEXT\LETTERS\OVERDUE.DOC
```

then the file is copied into the current directory.

Here are a few points to remember in copying files from one directory to another:

1. A file cannot be copied into the same directory under the same filename.
2. When the drive or path parameters are not specified in either the source or target files, the default drive and current directory are assumed.
3. If the filename is not specified for the target drive, the copied file will be given the same filename.
4. The use of global filename characters (wild cards) is permitted in both the source and target file specifications.
5. The /V parameter causes the COPY command to run slightly more slowly. This parameter has the same effect as the **VERIFY ON** command.
6. The COPY command also can be used to transfer data between any of the system devices. For example, the **COPY CON** command allows the user to create a file directly from the keyboard.

5.

File Management and Maintenance

A *File* is a collection of related data items. It is the basic unit of disk storage. Since a large number of files may be created and stored on the fixed disk, these files must be organized and maintained. Indeed, the key to making optimal use of the fixed disk is establishing a file management system.

A number of unique file management issues arise when an XT or AT is used. For example, a finite number of files can be stored on a fixed disk. In contrast, there is no theoretical limit to the number of files that can be used by a PC because an unlimited number of diskettes can be used. The fixed disk of the XT and AT is also likely to contain a number of different applications. As a result, the user of the XT and AT needs the ability to efficiently copy, backup, list, sort, combine, and remove files. In other words, the user must routinely organize and reorganize the fixed disk's logical file groupings.

This chapter introduces the user to file specifications, file types, and DOS features needed for managing and maintaining files.

5.1. File Specifications

Files in DOS are specified in the following format:

`[d:][filename].[extension]`

The parameters in this example have the following meaning:

d: This specifies the disk drive on which the file is resident.

filename   This is a name assigned by the user or the application. The filename may contain up to eight characters. In DOS, the valid characters include: all alpha characters, the values 0 through 9, and the following special characters:

$$ \$ \; \# \; \& \; @ \; ! \; \% \; (\;) \; — \; « \; » \; ` \; \_ \; ' \; ^ \; \sim $$

extension   This is an additional identifier that specifies the file type. It may be assigned by the user or automatically assigned by certain applications. The extension is separated from the filename by a period. There are no spaces between the filename and the extension. An extension may be up to three characters in length and can employ the same valid characters listed above.

Certain information should be kept in mind when assigning filenames and filename extensions:

1) Although the characters listed above are valid for naming DOS files, they may not be valid characters for other application programs that utilize the DOS operating system. For example, Lotus 1-2-3 does not allow the use of any characters except A through Z, 0 through 9, and the underscore (_). To ensure compatibility between DOS and application programs, it is a good idea initially to compare the filenaming restrictions of DOS and the various applications in use. Most application documentation should outline the filenaming rules.

2) If the user does not assign an eight-character filename or a three-character extension, DOS assigns a space character to the unused positions. Thus, DOS reads up to the first space that it encounters. For example: PERIOD.BAT is read as PERIOD<sp><sp>.BAT. The <sp> indicates a space character. In contrast, PERIOD is read as PERIOD <sp><sp>, with no filename extension.

    This feature of DOS permits the use of global filename characters in a number of ways. These are discussed in detail in Chapter 6.

3) Device names cannot be used as filenames. These include: AUX, COM#, CON, LPT#, NUL, and PRN. (Note: The # refers to the number of the device; e.g., Communications Port #2.)

4) DOS command names cannot be used as batch filenames. For example, the user cannot create a batch file called BACKUP.BAT. This is because BACKUP.COM is a DOS program file and will override the batch file when the command is issued. If the user types BACKUP, instead of executing the batch file by that name, DOS will respond with the error message:

`Invalid Number of Parameters`

5) The user should not assign certain filename extensions to applications files. These include .EXE, .COM, .$$$, and .BAK. These extensions are

reserved for program files (.EXE and .COM), temporary files (.$$$) and DOS backup files (.BAK). Other extensions have special meanings and must be assigned by the user in appropriate situations. Examples of these include .BAT for batch files and .BAS for BASIC files. Finally, some extensions are automatically assigned by an application program. For example, Lotus 1-2-3 automatically assigns the extension .PRN to print files and .WKS to worksheet files.

5.2. Directory and Filename Listings

The DOS directory serves as an index of files for the disk. As previously described in Chapter 4, a directory entry lists the filename and extension, the number of bytes in the file, and the date and time it was created:

Example 5–1.

```
DIR

Volume in drive C is XTMGMT

Directory of C:\


ANSI    SYS    1664   3-08-83    12:00p
```

Although this is what the user sees when the DIR command is issued, DOS stores much more information in a directory listing. Each directory entry is 32 bytes; the information contained in this entry is presented in Figure 5–1.

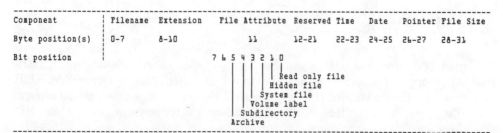

```
Directory Entry = 32 Bytes

------------------------------------------------------------------------
Component       | Filename  Extension   File Attribute  Reserved  Time   Date    Pointer  File Size
Byte position(s)| 0-7       8-10            11          12-21     22-23   24-25   26-27    28-31
Bit position    |                      7 6 5 4 3 2 1 0
                                         | | | | | | | |
                                         | | | | | | | |__Read only file
                                         | | | | | | |____Hidden file
                                         | | | | | |_____System file
                                         | | | | |_____Volume label
                                         | | | |_____Subdirectory
                                         Archive
------------------------------------------------------------------------
```

Figure 5–1. **Table of the various components of a 32-byte directory entry, listing byte positions for each component. Each bit of the File Attribute byte (11) indicates a file type or attribute; byte positions 12 through 21 are not being used by DOS at this time and are reserved for future use.**

As is evident in Figure 5–1, the directory entry contains data on the filename and extension, the time and date the file was created, and the file size (in bytes). Although it is not visible on the screen to the user, the first byte of the filename field includes the directory entry's status. DOS uses this status information to determine if:

1) the entry has ever been used
2) the entry was used but erased
3) the entry is a directory rather than a file

This information limits the length of directory searches and improves the performance of DOS.

In addition, the directory entry contains one byte specifying the file attributes and two bytes signifying pointer information. These latter two components warrant further discussion.

The file attribute (byte 11 in Figure 5–1) refers to the accessibility characteristics of the file. Each bit position in the file attribute byte signifies a different characteristic. For example, when all bits are off, it is termed a NORMAL file—one that is subject to normal DOS operations. In addition, the first bit signifies a file with READ-ONLY access; the second bit signifies a HIDDEN FILE; the third bit signifies a SYSTEM FILE; and the fourth bit signifies the VOLUME LABEL. Neither the hidden files nor the system files appear in the directory listing of a disk. Furthermore, internal DOS commands such as COPY and ERASE will not work on these files. Examples of these hidden system files are IBMBIO.COM and IBMDOS.COM; both files are essential components of the DOS operating system, and are "protected" as such.

The pointer information (in bytes 27 and 28) is essentially the link between the file entry in the directory and the File Allocation Table (FAT). The pointer indicates the "starting cluster" number for the file entry on the disk. The File Allocation Table converts the "clusters" to the sector numbers where the file will reside on the disk; i.e., it tells where on the disk the file can be found.

5.3. File Types

The user is confronted with a number of file types when working with DOS and other applications software. It is useful to distinguish between files that are program files and files that are created by the user. As described above, the file type is identified by the three-character extension of the file specification.

Command (.COM) files

COM files are machine language command files. Three essential DOS Command files are sent to Random Access Memory (RAM) every time DOS is loaded. These Command files are:

`IBMBIO.COM`

`IBMDOS.COM`

`COMMAND.COM`

The relationship between these three Command files and the initialization of DOS is presented in Figure 5–2. This figure illustrates how the three COM files listed above may be used.

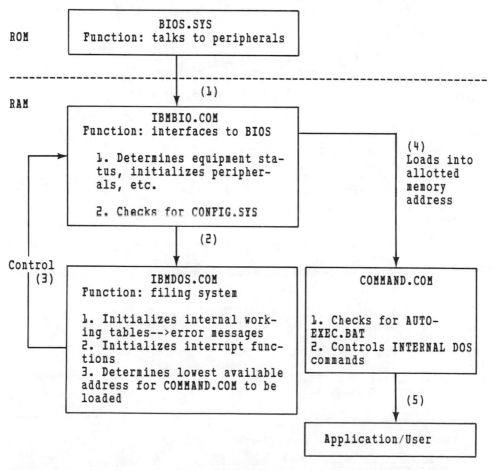

Figure 5–2. Diagram of essential DOS Command files and how each is involved in the initialization of DOS.

The function of IBMBIO.COM is to interface with the BIOS (Basic Input/Output System, located in Read-Only Memory). It determines equipment status, checks the system configuration devices, and initializes peripherals such as the printer. The IBMBIO.COM also loads the COMMAND.COM file into its allotted memory address.

IBMDOS.COM functions as a filing system. It initializes the internal working tables of DOS and its interrupt functions. It also determines the lowest available address for COMMAND.COM to be loaded into RAM.

COMMAND.COM controls the internal DOS commands. These are frequently-used DOS commands that are kept in RAM, the computer's temporary memory. Examples of such internal commands are COPY, ERASE, DIRECTORY (DIR), CHANGE DIRECTORY (CD), and TYPE. However, COMMAND.COM does not control external DOS commands. External commands must be loaded into memory from a disk whenever they are issued by the user. Each external command is its own program file. See Figure 5–3 for a listing of DOS program files, including a breakdown of its internal and external commands.

```
          DOS Program Files:  External Commands
          ---------------------------------------------

COMMAND (.COM) Files                     EXECUTABLE (.EXE) Files
-----------------------------------------------------------------------

    ASSIGN    DISKCOPY   PRINT      :    EXE2BIN
    BACKUP    EDLIN      RECOVER    :    FIND
    CHKDSK    FDISK      RESTORE    :    LINK
    COMMAND   FORMAT     SYS        :    SORT
    COMP      GRAPHICS   TREE       :
    DEBUG     MODE                  :
    DISKCOMP  MORE                  :
                                    :

========================================================================

                   DOS Internal Commands
                   ---------------------

    BATCH     DIR      PATH      SHIFT
    BREAK     ECHO     PAUSE     TIME
    CHDIR     ERASE    PROMPT    TYPE
    CLS       FOR      REM       VER
    COPY      GOTO     RENAME    VERIFY
    CTTY      IF       RMDIR     VOL
    DATE      MKDIR    SET

---------------------------------------------------------------------
```

Figure 5–3. DOS External and Internal program files.

Executable (.EXE) files

EXE files are executable DOS files that are written in binary notation. DOS contains four EXE files: FIND, LINK, SORT, and EXE2BIN. All are external DOS commands. When the user issues a DOS command, DOS searches the disk for a file with that command name and a .COM extension; if a .COM file by that name is not found, DOS then searches for the same filename with an .EXE extension. Thus, EXE files serve as DOS second-order command files that are used less frequently than their COM file counterparts.

System (.SYS) files

SYS files are files that are used by the operating system. They hold software routines that control and communicate with the system's devices or peripherals. DOS includes the file ANSI.SYS. This file contains the American National Standards Institute set of terminal codes (standard codes for controlling the video screen). The ANSI.SYS command instructs DOS to replace the standard screen and keyboard functions with extended screen and keyboard functions.

The user may create his or her own CONFIG.SYS file. This special configuration file is checked by DOS when the system is booted and is used to set the following DOS commands:

BREAK = ON/OFF	The default value is "OFF." Setting this command to ON instructs DOS to check for a Ctrl-Break whenever a program invokes a DOS function. OFF causes Ctrl-Break to be recognized only in standard Input/Output situations.
BUFFERS = xx	The number of BUFFERS (xx) may be set between 1 and 99. A buffer is a block of memory that is allocated to hold data being written to and from a disk. When part of a program file is read, DOS brings portions of the file into the buffer. Similarly, when information is written to the disk, it first is held in the disk buffer. This is a particularly useful command when using programs that frequently read and write to various portions of a file. Increasing the number of buffers will speed up the read/write process, up to a point.
DEVICE =	This specifics the name of a file containing a device driver. For example:

```
DEVICE=ANSI.SYS
```

FILES = xx

A device driver is a hardware-specific program to which DOS transfers control when accessing that hardware.

A value up to 99 may be entered. This command sets the maximum number of files that may be opened at any one time. The default value, 8, is sufficient for most uses. This value may have to be increased if the user is programming an application that requires more than 8 files to be opened at one time.

SHELL =

The DOS program includes the command processor COMMAND.COM. The SHELL command allows the user to specify a command processor that will be used in lieu of COMMAND.COM. The SHELL command is probably more often used to move the COMMAND.COM file from a fixed disk's root directory to a subdirectory. For example, the command

```
SHELL=COMMAND.COM C:\PROGRAMS
```

places the command processor in a subdirectory called PROGRAMS, and COMMAND.COM is accessed through the path:

```
C:\PROGRAMS\COMMAND.COM.
```

That is, it instructs the system to look into the subdirectory C:\PROGRAMS for COMMAND.COM.

Batch (.BAT) files

Batch files are user-created files containing one or more commands that can be executed by DOS. These commands are automatically executed in a program-like fashion when the user types the name of the batch file at the system prompt. In order for DOS to recognize these auto-command files, the file specification must contain a .BAT extension. When an existing batch file is edited with the DOS Line or Text Editor (EDLIN), DOS automatically creates a backup file and gives it the extension .BAK. Batch files are discussed in detail in Chapters 7 and 8.

Other File Types

A number of other file types can be found in various applications software. As described above, the extension of the filename specification identifies the file type. For example, some common extensions that the user might encounter are:

BAS   A BASIC program file.

PRN   A print or standard text file that is in ASCII format. Unlike a binary file (e.g., .COM and .EXE files), a .PRN file may be displayed at the system level using the TYPE command.

WKS   A Worksheet file in Lotus 1-2-3. The applications software automatically assigns the .WKS extension when the file is saved.

DOC   A Document file in MultiMate and other word processing software. The applications software automatically assigns the .DOC extension when the file is saved.

$$$ A temporary or incorrectly stored file. This might be the case if only a portion of a file were saved.

@@@   This type of file is most often seen when using the DOS BACKUP command. The BACKUP command places a file with the extension .$$$ on each backup disk. This file records the sequential disk number.

5.4. Global Filename Characters

Global filename characters are symbols that can be used to refer to any characters that occupy specified positions in a filename. Global filename characters may be used with DOS commands to specify groups of files rather than individual files. DOS provides the user with two global filename characters or "wild cards": the asterisk and the question mark. Global filename characters are extrordinarily useful tools when used with a variety of DOS's file management-related commands.

The ? Global Filename Character

Use of the ? wild card in a filename or extension means that any character can occupy the position. Each ? must match one character.

─────────────*Example 5–2.*─────────────

The command DIR DATA??84.WKS will list specific Lotus 1-2-3 filenames. The filenames must meet ALL of the following criteria:

1) Filenames begin with the word DATA.
2) The word DATA in the filenames is followed by two characters.
3) Filenames end with the characters 84.
4) The extension is .WKS.

In the above example, global filename characters would be useful for producing a list of data files by month. For example, the command DIR DATA??84.WKS might produce the following directory listing:

DATA0184.WKS

DATA0284.WKS

DATA0384.WKS

⋮

⋮

DATA1284.WKS

The * Global Filename Character

The * wild card is used to indicate that one or more characters can occupy specified positions in a filename. The * must, however, always be used at the end of a filename or filename extension. For example, the command

DIR DATA*.WKS

is a valid command. But the commands

DIR *84.WKS   and   DIR DATA*84.WKS

are invalid commands.

_____ *Example 5–3.* _____

COPY *.WKS A:	All Lotus 1-2-3 files in the current directory (.WKS files) are copied from the current directory to a floppy diskette in the A drive.
COPY DATA*.WKS A:	All 1-2-3 filenames in the current directory that begin with the word "DATA" are copied to the A drive. All filenames are selected regardless of the number of characters that come after the word "DATA" in the filename.
COPY *.* A:	All files in the current directory are copied to the A drive.

An exception to the use of * and ? can be found with the DIR command. When the DIR command is issued with a filename but no extension, all filename extensions on the current drive are implied.

─────────────────────────**Example 5–4.**─────────────────────────

Issuing the command DIR DATA0184 might produce the listing:

```
DATAO184.WKS

DATAO184.PRN

DATAO184.BAS
```

This is the same as entering the command as DIR DATA0184.*.

Similarly, if the DIR command is issued with an extension but no file-name, all filenames on the current drive are implied.

─────────────────────────**Example 5–5.**─────────────────────────

Issuing the command DIR .WKS might produce the listing:

```
DATAO184.WKS

DATAO284.WKS

DATAO384.WKS
```

5.5. Combining and Comparing Files

DOS provides a number of commands that allow the user to organize and manipulate a collection of files at the system level. These commands allow the user to combine, compare, rename, sort, display, and search for files.

As discussed in the previous chapter, the establishment of subdirectories allows the user to structure his or her file library in manageable chunks. These commands may be used to manipulate the way files are stored between and within subdirectories.

Combining Data Files

A lesser known function of the COPY command is its file combination or concatenation facility. Using conventional file specifications, several of the COPY command switches, and "+" signs, any number of files may be linked together. Combining files using the COPY command uses the following format:

```
COPY [/A][/B][d:][path][source filename 1[.ext]][/A][/B]+

    [/A][/B][d:][path][source filename n[.ext]][/A][/B]

    [/A][/B][d:][path][target filename[.ext]][/A][/B][/V]
```

The parameters in this command have the following meanings:

d:	The drive specification for each file.
path	The path parameter guides DOS to the appropriate level in the directory system for the specified files.
filename	The "source" files are the files to be combined (1 . . . n). The "target" file is the file containing the linked files.
+	The filename specification that follows the "+" is added to the previously specified filename.
/A	This signifies an ASCII file.
/B	This signifies a binary file.
/V	This switch verifies that sectors written to in the target file are recorded intact.

Using the /A and /B Switches

The placement and use of the /A and /B switches are crucial to the command's outcome:

1) A switch following the COPY command, thus preceding all file specifications, sets the switch globally for all files in the command. For example, the command

   COPY /A C:SOURCE1.PRN+C:SOURCE2.PRN C:TARGET.PRN

   indicates that the three files are ASCII files. The command combines the contents of the two .PRN files, SOURCE1 and SOURCE2, in the .PRN file, TARGET.PRN. The /A switch is the default setting when combining files with the COPY command.

2) A switch following a filename refers to that filename and all other filenames until the next switch is encountered. Consider the following command:

   COPY SOURCE1.PRN/A+SOURCE2.PRN+SOURCE3.PRN/B TARGET.PRN

   The above command sets the /A switch for the files named SOURCE1 and SOURCE2. When the /B switch is encountered following SOURCE3, that file (SOURCE3) and TARGET are defined as Binary (or /B) files.

3) The /A and the /B switches have different meanings when they refer to source and target files. These differences are outlined in Table 5–1. Basically, the switches can be used to control how the COPY command uses and reads the end-of-file marker (the symbols ^Z). Consider the following command:

```
COPY /A C:SOURCE1.PRN/A+C:SOURCE2.PRN/B  C:TARGET.PRN/A
```

This command copies SOURCE1 as an ASCII file, copies the entire SOURCE2 file (ignoring any ^Z characters), and places the combined results in the file, TARGET, which now ends with a ^Z character.

Table 5–1.

Switch	Source File	Target File
/A	Treats the referent file as an ASCII file. It tells DOS to copy up to the end-of-file marker (^Z).	Places an end-of-file marker (^Z) after the last character in the file.
/B	Copies the ENTIRE Binary file and ignores the ^Z character (which might be embedded in the middle of the Binary file).	No end-of-file character (^Z) is added to the file.

Combining Files into a Summary File

The conventional format of the COPY command,

```
COPY C:SOURCE1.PRN+C:SOURCE2.PRN C:TARGET.PRN
```

combines the source files into a new or existing summary file. In the example given here, all of the files are ASCII files because the /A switch is the default setting. Such an outcome of the COPY command might be useful for file archiving purposes. Or, a number of print (.PRN) files can be combined into a single print file for uploading to a mainframe system.

——————————————*Example 5–6.*——————————————

A spreadsheet application using Lotus 1-2-3 is developed that calculates interest for 2400 customer loans. A mailing address is maintained with each customer's record. Since there is such a large customer base, the 2400 customer records are divided alphabetically into eight files of 300 customers each. To expediently produce mailing addresses with interest amounts, extracted data from each file are converted from binary format (Lotus 1-2-3

.WKS files) to print (.PRN) files. Using the COPY command, the resulting print files can be combined into a single .PRN ASCII file and uploaded to a mainframe.

In the above example, the following COPY command might be used:

```
COPY INT0181A.PRN+INT0181B.PRN+INT0181C.PRN+

     INT0181D.PRN+INT0181E.PRN+INT0181F.PRN

     SINT0181.PRN/V
```

The files INT0181A.PRN, etc. refer to January 1981 interest for group A, B, and so on. The file SINT0181.PRN refers to summary interest for January 1981. A single file, the interest summary file (SINT0181.PRN) is uploaded to the mainframe. Both the default drive (C:\) and the default switch setting (/A) are assumed in the above example.

Combining Files into the Original Source File

When no target file is specified, the COPY command combines all of the source files into the first source file specified. The DOS COPY command, in effect, sequentially chains subsequent source files to the first source file. Thus, the command

```
COPY C:SOURCE1.PRN+C:SOURCE2.PRN+C:SOURCE3.PRN
```

results in the combination of all three files being stored in the SOURCE1.PRN file.

────────────────── *Example 5–7.* ──────────────────

An author prepares a book chapter manuscript using word processing software. Additions to the chapter are prepared at a later date in different text files. The author wishes to combine the additions with the original chapter text.

In the above example, the following COPY command might be used:

```
COPY C:CHAPTER3.TXT+C:CH3PART2.TXT+C:CH3PART3.TXT
```

This command sequentially adds Parts II and III to Chapter 3. The result is a complete chapter file named CHAPTER3.TXT.

Changing the Time and Date of a File

When DOS is used to copy a file, the time and date are not changed in the directory entry. Under some circumstances, the user may want the copied file to show a current time and date.

————————————————————————Example 5–8.————————————————————————

Consider again the previous example in which several files were appended to the original source file (CHAPTER3.TXT). Here, the COPY command can be used to update the date and time of CHAPTER3.TXT. This provides the author with a record of when the files were appended.

The following COPY command might be used to simply change the time and date:

```
COPY C:CHAPTER3.TXT+,, C:
```

In this example, two commas are used to define the end of the source file-name (CHAPTER3.TXT). Otherwise, DOS would expect another source file-name to follow the "+" sign.

Comparing Files

The COMP command is used to make comparisons between two files. This command is used most often to ensure that a copy of a file is identical to a source file. The two files must have different names if they are contained in the same directory. However, files to be compared may have the same file-name if they are located on different disks or in separate directories. The COMP command uses the following format:

```
COMP d:[path][filename][.ext] d:[path][filename][.ext]
```

Each of the parameters follows the standard definitions described in the previous examples. DOS refers to the first file specification as the PRIMARY file and the second file as the SECONDARY file. If only the COMP command, or just the COMP command plus the primary file specification are entered, DOS will prompt the user for additional parameters (see Figure 5–4 for COMP command messages).

Note: With DOS 3.X, the parameter [d:][path] may be placed in front of the command. Since COMP is an external command, this allows the user to specify the particular drive and directory in which the command file is located. The pathname is separated from the command by a backslash (\).

Message	*Explanation*
Compare error at off-set XXXXXXXX	The files that are being compared contain different values at the offset displayed in the hexidecimal notation (the XXX's).
Compare more files (Y/N)?	The previous comparison is complete. A "Y" response results in the next two prompts discussed below.
Enter primary file name	The "Primary" file is the first file to be compared. This prompt follows either (1) the issuance of the COMP command without any specifications or (2) the "Compare more files (Y)?" message.
Enter 2nd file name or drive id	The "Secondary" file is the other half of the comparison. This message appears when either the COMP command is issued without any specifications or the secondary file parameter is not specified. Only the drive name (e.g., c:\) need be specified if the filename is identical for both files.
EOF mark not found	If the last byte of a file being compared is not ^Z (end-of-file marker), this message is not displayed. This message is used because some products produce directory entries in multiples of 128 bytes rather than showing actual file size. A search by DOS with the COMP command allows the two files to be compared anyway.
File AND File	Gives the full path and filenames under comparison.
Files are different sizes	The two files to be compared are not the same size. The COMP command cannot be used.
Files compare OK	The two files under comparison contain identical information.
10 mismatches— ending comparison	At least 10 mismatched locations were found in the files under comparison. COMP terminates under the assumption that further comparisons are useless.

Figure 5–4. COMP command system and error messages.

DOS also allows the user to compare more than one set of files at a time. This is done using the COMP command with global filename characters or wild cards. For example, the user could compare all of the files in one directory with all files in a duplicate backup directory. When more than one set of files is compared, DOS displays the paths and filenames as the comparison proceeds.

Nine different system and error messages are produced with the COMP command. One aspect of the COMP command that should be remembered is that the COMP command does not produce the pause prompt:

`Strike a key when ready...`

Thus, if the data to be compared are on a separate disk from the primary file, the user should first enter just the command COMP (without any parameters), and then respond to each of the system prompts.

5.6. Sorting and Searching for Filenames and File Contents

DOS provides the user with three types of filters that are particularly useful for manipulating file listings. A *Filter* is a command or program that transforms input data and outputs the results to a device such as a printer or a file. Included as external commands in DOS's advanced versions are the filters FIND, MORE, and SORT. FIND and SORT will be discussed in the following sections.

The FIND Filter

FIND searches for all occurrences of a particular string in each of the filenames specified. It also includes three switches that can be activated to provide the user with basic data on the number, placement, and contents of matching and mismatching lines.

The FIND Format

The FIND filter is used with the following format:

`FIND [/C][/N][/V]"string"[d:] [path][filename][.ext]...`

The switches /C, /N, and /V MUST precede the string. The string also must be enclosed in double quotes. Single switches may be specified or combinations of switches may be used. The switches have the following meaning:

/C	Displays a count of the number of matched lines.
/N	Displays the line number and contents of each matching line.
/V	Displays all mismatched line contents.
/C/V	Displays a count of the number of mismatched lines.
/N/V	Displays the line number and contents of each nonmatching line.

Note: With DOS 3.X, the parameter [d:][path] may be placed in front of the command. Since FIND is an external command, this allows the user to specify the particular drive and directory in which the command file is located. The pathname is separated from the command by a backslash (\).

Use of the FIND Filter

The FIND filter can be most useful for examining the common contents of a number of files.

_____ *Example 5–9.* _____

The FIND command could be used to search through a number of text or word processing files to locate all references to a particular client. The following command:

```
FIND /N"Silicon Megasystems" CLIENTS1.TXT CLIENTS2.TXT

    CLIENTS3.TXT CLIENTS4.TXT CLIENTS5.TXT
```

would search through the five files (CLIENTS1 . . . 5.TXT) and display the line number and contents of all lines that contain the client name, Silicon Megasystems.

_____

In the above example, the path is omitted and the current drive is assumed to be the default drive. By using the command described in the above example, the user would not have to display or print the entire contents of each of the five files.

One also can use the FIND command to locate all files in a directory listing that contain a particular word or series of characters:

_____ *Example 5–10.* _____

A user produces monthly updates of financial data under separate filenames. Each filename contains the month number (e.g., "01," "02," etc.) and the year ("84" or "1984"). The user desires to produce a listing of all files for the year, 1984. Unfortunately, the "84" can appear in any of the eight filename positions (e.g., DATA0184.WKS or 0284SUM.WKS), thus making global filename characters unusable. The FIND command can be used to perform a search of the directory listing:

```
DIR¦ FIND/N"84"
```

Using the command sequence presented above, the output would be those directory listings in which the filename contained the sequence "84." This also would include "1984" listings.

Note that the symbol " ¦ " is used to chain together the DIR and FIND commands. This ¦ symbol illustrates the use of DOS's Piping features. *Piping* refers to the chaining together of DOS commands such that standard inputs and outputs are automatically redirected. In the above example, the ¦ symbol passes the output of the DIR command through the FIND filter before it is displayed on the screen. The FIND filter in this example specifies that only files containing "84" should be displayed. For further information on DOS's piping features, refer to information on DOS advanced commands in the DOS 2.X and 3.X Reference Manuals.

Limitations of the FIND Filter

Although the FIND filter is a powerful tool, it has several limitations:

1) Global filename characters are not permitted in filenames and extensions. Thus, if one wants to search through the text of a number of files, each filename and extension must be specified. One may get around this limitation by using FIND in a batch file with the FOR batch command (see Chapter 8).

2) The FIND filter is ASCII-based and searches only for exact matches. This means that upper- and lower-case letters, for example, have different ASCII representations and are treated differently. Using "The" as the string to be matched would produce different results from using the string "the." Searching for company names (e.g., Silicon Megasystems in the previous example) would produce less ambiguous results because company names usually start with capital letters, regardless of their position in a sentence.

The SORT Filter

The SORT command reads information from an input device, sorts it in ascending (A to Z) alphabetical order, and sends it to an output device. The SORT command also includes two switches that sort information in descending (Z to A) alphabetical order and perform a sort using a specified column as the primary sort key.

The SORT Format

The SORT filter is used with the following format:

```
SORT [/R][/+n]
```

The two switches, /R and /+n, are used either as single switches or in combination; they must precede the input source.

> **/R**   Sorts the information in descending (Z to A) alphabetical order.
>
> **/+n** The primary sort key is set to start at column "n"; the default is column 1. For example, setting this switch as /+14 when sorting a directory listing produces a list of directory entries in file size order.

Note: With DOS 3.X, the parameter [d:][path] may be placed in front of the command. Since SORT is an external command, this allows the user to specify the particular drive and directory in which the command file is located. The pathname is separated from the command by a backslash (\).

Use of the SORT Filter

The SORT command can accept keyboard input as its source and typically outputs information to the video display.

Example 5–11.

If only the SORT command is issued at the DOS prompt, the cursor moves to the beginning of the next line to accept keyboard input. Suppose the user enters the SORT command and then enters the following list:

```
text

chapters

examples

index

graphs

tables

contents
```

When a "Control Z" character (the [F6] key or end-of-file marker) is entered, DOS will sort the list in ascending alphabetical order, beginning with "chapters" and ending with "text."

However, this use of SORT is not the most efficient if one must continually update and alphabetize the file contents. Typically, SORT is used with another file as the input device:

Example 5–12.

The SORT command can be used to aphabetize a list of index items contained in the file INDEX.TXT. The sorted output then can be directed to the printer. If the command sequence

```
SORT <INDEX.TXT >PRN
```

is issued, the index file is sorted in alphabetical order and sent to the printer.

Note the use of the < > symbols in the above example. The "less than" (<) sign indicates the redirection of INPUT to the specified device. Thus, the command SORT <INDEX.TXT tells DOS to take the input from the file named INDEX.TXT and sort its contents. The "greater than" sign (>) indicates the redirection of the OUTPUT to the specified device. In this case, >PRN means that the output (the alphabetized index file) should be directed to the printer instead of the video display.

Other DOS commands also can be filtered through the SORT filter using DOS's Piping features:

Example 5–13.

An alphabetized directory listing can be obtained using the DIR and SORT commands:

```
DIR ¦ SORT
```

The results of this command would appear on the video display since no redirection of the output device is specified.

Note that the SORT command in the previous example does not permanently alter the order of the directory listing. Subsequent issuance of the DIR command alone would produce an unalphabetized directory listing.

Limitations of the SORT Filter

Just as was the case with the FIND filter, the SORT filter has its limitations as well:

1) The maximum file size that can be sorted is 63,000 characters.
2) File contents are sorted in ASCII sequence. Thus, capital letters will always precede lower-case letters. For example, in a computer book index file, capitalized DOS commands such as "TYPE" would always appear at the top of the list rather than in true alphabetical sequence.

3) Numeric sequences other than 0 through 9 cannot be sorted because numbers in ASCII files are treated as characters. For example, the list of numbers: 10 20 30 40 50 100 200, would be sorted as: 10 100 20 200 30 40 50.

4) The end-of-file marker, Control-Z, appears before alphanumeric characters in a listing of ASCII characters. When SORT is used with a file containing the ^Z character, and the result is output to a file, the resulting file cannot be edited or typed out. This is because the DOS command TYPE, for example, reads the end-of-file marker and fails to recognize that additional lines in the file come after the ^Z.

5.7. A Summary of Useful Information on DOS Files

1. Files are specified with the filename (eight character limitation) followed by a period (.) and a three-character extension that specifies the file type.

2. If a full eight-character filename or a three-character extension is not specified, DOS assigns a space character to the unused positions. This feature permits the use of Global Filenames or wild cards: ? and *.

3. The directory entry contains data on the filename and the extension, the time and date the file was created, and the file size. DOS uses the first position of the filename field to determine the following:

    A. Whether the entry has ever been used.
    B. Whether the entry was used but erased.
    C. Whether the entry was a directory or a file.

    This information limits the length of directory searches and improves DOS performance.

4. Different file types will be encountered by the user: Command (.COM) files, Executable (.EXE) DOS files, System (.SYS) files, user-created executable or Batch (.BAT) files, and application-specific files.

5. Files can be combined using the COPY command. Two files can be combined together into the original source file, or two files can be added together into a new file. The COPY command also can be used to change the time and date of a copied file.

6. The COMP command is used to compare two files. Most often, this command is used to ensure that a copy of the file is identical to the source file. COMP also can be used with global filename characters to compare more than one pair of files. For example, all files in one directory can be compared with files in a duplicate or backup directory.

7. The FIND command is used to search for all exact occurrences of a particular string in specified files. The FIND command's switches can be used to produce information on the number of lines in a file that

contain a match or a mismatch and the line number and contents of each matching or mismatching line.

8. The SORT command can be used to sort information into ascending or descending alphabetical order. Maximum file size to be sorted is 63,000 characters. File contents are sorted in ASCII sequences. Numeric sequences other than 0 through 9 cannot be sorted because numbers in ASCII files are treated as characters.

6.

Filenaming Conventions

Filenaming conventions refer to a general agreement on the usage of filenames to identify and describe the contents of files. These rules or standards for naming files provide the user with a tool that increases the efficiency of file management and takes the guesswork out of file identification.

Filenaming conventions are best established at the time the machine is first installed. This allows one to define a scheme that can be easily understood by multiple users. Thus, users can name new files in accordance with the filenaming conventions; more importantly, they can easily locate and identify preexisting files. As the volume of files increases over time, filenaming standards will reduce the amount of time required to perform many managerial tasks associated with disk organization and file maintenance.

This chapter describes the significance of filenaming conventions and provides some guidelines on how they might be used. Sample filenaming schemes and uses are presented throughout the chapter; they illustrate the benefits of filenaming conventions and suggest how filenaming conventions might be made more accessible to the user.

6.1. Designing Filenaming Conventions

Filenaming conventions can be designed in a number of different ways, depending on the needs of the end user and the various types of applications. For example, if there are multiple users, it may be necesary to use a unique ID within the filename to identify the "owner" of the data. Similarly, if files contain time-dependent data (e.g., daily financial data), the month, day, and year may be critical to a file's identification. At the time the machine is installed, thought must be given to:

1. The number and needs of different users.
2. The number and types of different applications.
3. Any time dependencies of data files (e.g., must the filename contain either the day, month, or year?).

4. The compatibility between the filename characters used in DOS and other software.
5. The relationship between filenaming conventions and the establishment of tree-structured directories and subdirectories.

Utilizing Column Positions in the Filename

Perhaps the best way of establishing filenaming conventions is to assign meaning to each of the eight column positions in a filename. As described in the previous chapter, DOS allows the user to assign up to eight characters in a filename and three characters in an extension. Since extensions are often assigned by particular programs or software applications, it is advisable to restrict the filenaming conventions to the filename itself.

In order to design a filenaming scheme using column positions, a number of decisions have to be made. Most importantly, the user must decide how to categorize application types (and subtypes, if necessary). Once types and subtypes have been identified, each one must be assigned a unique code. This code can be either alphabetic or numeric. The main deciding factor here is the code's mnemonic characteristics, or its ability to trigger meaningfulness to the user. For example, use of the letter "I" to indicate an interest payment file has more meaning to the user than file type "5," which also might signify an interest payment file.

The user must also decide the detail level that he or she wants to build into the filename. For example, a filename could simply indicate that the file is a memo written on a particular date. Or, the filename could contain a reference number to indicate the subject of the memo, the recipient of the memo, and so on.

In designing a filenaming scheme, it is important to construct it with enough flexibility so that more detail may be added at a later time. This could be accomplished by including several "open" positions within the eight-column limitation. When not necessary to the identification of a file, the position(s) could always contain the number "0." If this type of strategy is used, the detail level of the filenaming scheme can be easily modified. Another code number or letter can be added rather than adding or deleting the position itself.

Finally, the user must decide on a logical order of the codes for the various column positions. This order must be consistent for all files on the hard disk. The user then is able to gain maximum benefit from DOS file management features such as directory sorts and global filename characters. This order also should be meaningful to the user. For example, if the most critical identifier of the data files is application type, then this code should precede all others.

————————————————————————————————*Example 6–1.*————————————————————————————————

The hard disk of an AT is organized into five general categories based upon the type of the file. These types include:

> Documents
> Financial Data
> Models
> Tracking Systems
> Client Information

Each one of these categories can further be subdivided into three or more subtypes:

(D)ocuments	(F)inancial Data
- (L)etter	- (F)ees Receivable
- (M)emo	- (I)nterest Receivable
- (N)arrative	- (M)ortgage Payments
(M)odels	(T)racking Systems
- (B)udget Analysis	- (D)ates
- (C)redit Analysis	- (E)mployees
- (M)arketing Models	- (P)rojects

> (C)lient Data
>   - (A)ddresses
>   - (C)redit Information
>   - (M)arketing Data

Thus, the file filenaming codes for budget models would be "MB"; for addresses of clients, "CA," etc.

In the above example, suppose that the date of each file's creation is important to each application. In addition, assume that multiple users of the AT require that the user of each file be identified as well. Given the organization of the hard disk by file type and the requirements for user ID and date information, filenaming conventions can be established. Each of the eight column positions of the filename can be coded to uniquely identify the contents of each type and version of a file:

Position #	Information
1	File type
2	File subtype
3	Month 1
4	Month 2
5	Year 1
6	Year 2
7	User ID
8	Open position

Note that in the preceding coding structure, two positions were allocated for the month and the year. For example, July 1984 could be represented as "0784."

Using the specifications outlined in the example above, files on the hard disk can now be identified by type and subtype. The user also has cues as to the identification of the information on the file. For example:

FF0785N0　　Indicates that this is a financial data file containing fees receivable information. It contains the fees receivable for July 1985, and the user is Nancy Cain. Note that the last position contains a "0," indicating that this position is not used.

TP0885T0　　Indicates that this is a project tracking system created by Tom Cain in August 1985.

In the above example, some aspects of the filenaming strategy might require more detail. For example, it may not be very useful to the user to know simply that a file contains a memo written in July of 1985; thirty or forty memos could have been written during that time period. As mentioned above, knowing the needs of the user is the key to organizing the filenaming scheme. Consider a second example that provides much greater detail:

—————————————— *Example 6–2.* ——————————————

Suppose in the previous example that "Type" is defined differently. If each type specified in the first example is set up as a separate directory (e.g., \TRACKING), then another filenaming strategy can be used that provides far greater detail.

Consider a series of files for tracking principal, interest, and fee amounts accrued on a quarterly basis. The amounts can be accrued in one of four different currencies and the interest rate (pricing) can be either a domestic or non-domestic source. This produces the following structure:

Position #	Information
1	File type: (F)ees, (I)nterest, (P)rincipal
2	Currency: (U)S$, (C)anadian$, (L)ira, (G)uilder
3	Pricing: (D)omestic, (N)on-domestic
4	Month 1: (0,1)
5	Month 2: (1–9)
6	Year 1: (0,9)
7	Year 2: (0,9)
8	Open Position

In the above example, the user has a good idea of the type of data in the file by simply looking at the filename. For example:

IUD06840   Indicates that this is an interest file containing amounts in US dollars, priced with a domestic source of funds. It contains data for the June 1984 payments. Note that the last position contains a "0," indicating that the open position is not used.

Another advantage of the above filenaming scheme is that DOS functions can be used to sort all files on the hard disk by currency, pricing, or type. For example, all files could be listed that contain Canadian dollar interest amounts. DOS functions such as SORT and FIND can be extraordinarily powerful file management tools when used in conjunction with filenaming conventions.

Using Meaningful Syllables in the Filename

An alternative to using column positions to establish a filename convention scheme is to use short, meaningful syllables within the filename. Thus, documentation files may be labelled "DOC," model-related files "MOD," and so on. For example, a file containing fees accrued for the month of March 1984 might be called "FEES0384." Meaningful syllables can be used very effectively under certain circumstances:

1. When all files to be stored on the hard disk are known at the onset; therefore, a great deal of flexibility for handling new filenames is not required.
2. When they are used in conjunction with a highly organized, many-layered, tree-structured directory. In this case, files can be organized into directories and subdirectories by file type, subtype, date, and so on. If the tree-structured directory contains too many levels, however, DOS search and retrieval time will be quite sluggish.

3. The meaningful syllable always appears in the same column positions for each filename. This permits the use of DOS utilities with global filename characters.

The greatest advantage of using this type of filenaming convention is that the first-time user can readily recognize filenames and identify file contents. Extensive documentation on the meaning of each filename column position is not required.

_____*Example 6–3.*_____

Consider the fifteen file types and subtypes outlined in Example 6–1. Instead of using letters to signify what each position means, short meaningful syllables could be established. For example:

MEMO0000 = A file containing a memo
LETR0000 = A file containing a letter
NARR0000 = A file containing a narrative text
INTP0000 = A file containing interest payment data
FEES0000 = A file containing fee accrual data
MORT0000 = A file containing mortgage payment data

_____

In the above example, the date, the financial quarter, or the user's initials could be placed in the remaining four positions to provide additional information. For example:

FEES0785 Indicates a file containing fees accrued for the month of July, 1985.

The greatest disadvantage of this type of filenaming scheme is that it breaks down when additional information is required in the filename. Hence, this type of scheme should only be used under the circumstances described above.

Using Filenames of Standard Lengths

In the examples described in this chapter, filenames have been designed to use each of the eight available character positions. This was done to ensure that global filename characters could be used for all files on the hard disk. Although some application filenames require fewer than eight characters, zeros or blanks (_) should be added to make each filename eight characters long. The logic behind the use of standard filename lengths is evident in the following example:

―――――――――――――――――――――――*Example 6-4.*――――――――――――――――――――――

All interest payment files stored on an AT have filenames that begin with the letter "I" and end with the year "84." However, the filenames are of various lengths, ranging from five to eight characters. Suppose that the user wants to copy all interest files for the year 1984 to a floppy disk (from Drive C to Drive A). With standard-length filenames, this could accomplished using the COPY command and global filename characters:

```
COPY C:\I?????84.* A:
```

However, since some of the filenames on this AT have less than eight characters (e.g., IU0784.WKS), these files will not be picked up by the command described above. In order to copy those files with six-character filenames, the command would have to be written as:

```
COPY C:\I??84.* A:
```

In the above example, the user would have to issue a separate COPY command for each filename length. This diminishes the effectiveness of using global filename characters.

6.2. Using Filenaming Conventions

In the previous section, filenaming conventions were described and several design strategies were presented. A carefully designed filenaming scheme is essential to a well-organized XT or AT system for three reasons:

1. Filenaming conventions allow the user to sort his or her directories and obtain an inventory of relevant files. For example, if date information is included in the filenaming scheme, sorting the directory will provide a list by file type in the date order. Although DOS includes its own date information in the directory listing, the date changes with each update to a file. In contrast, the date information in the filename always reflects the creation or start date of a file.
2. Well-designed filenaming conventions describe and/or abstract the contents of a file such that it is meaningful to multiple users. Filenaming conventions also provide a framework for naming subsequently-created files.
3. Filenaming conventions greatly increase the efficiency of file management and maintenance if they are used in conjunction with DOS commands and global filename characters.

To illustrate the importance of the above statements, several examples are presented below. For the purposes of these examples, assume that the following filenaming scheme has been designed (from Example 6–2):

Position #	Information
1	File type: (F)ees, (I)nterest, (P)rincipal
2	Currency: (U)S$, (C)anadian$, (L)ira, (G)uilder
3	Pricing: (D)omestic, (N)on-domestic
4	Month 1: (0,1)
5	Month 2: (1-9)
6	Year 1: (0,9)
7	Year 2: (0,9)
8	Open Position

Example: Use of Global Filename Characters

The user wants to move all interest files for 1985 from a subdirectory called INTEREST into a subdirectory containing only interest data for 1985 (called INTER85). The following command is issued:

```
COPY C:\interest\I????85?.*  C:\inter84
```

Using the ? global filename character, the user must include only the alphabetic code for file type ("I") and the year ("85") in the command specification. If, for example, 50 or more files are included in this population, performing this function without using global filename characters could be a highly time-consuming process.

Example: Archiving Files

Since the AT fixed disk has a limited capacity of 20 megabytes, it is useful to periodically archive unused or outdated files on a floppy diskette. Suppose that the user wants to archive all interest data for the month of July 1984. This could be accomplished by using the following command:

```
BACKUP C:\I??0784?.* A:
```

All data meeting these criteria would be copied onto a floppy diskette. If necessary, they could be restored to the fixed disk at a later time.

After these data are archived, it is desirable to erase all of the unused files from the fixed disk to free up storage space. This also can be accomplished using the ? global filename character:

```
ERASE C:\I??0784?.*
```

Once again, these two processes could be highly time-consuming if it were necessary to issue the same commands for each individual file.

6.3. The Advantages and Disadvantages of Filenaming Conventions

Although the advantages of using filenaming conventions far outweigh the disadvantages, naming conventions do have some disadvantages. Primarily, establishing a filenaming scheme up front takes a significant amount of time and vision. In many ways, the process is similar to building a well-constructed database. The amount of time and effort spent up front in the planning stage buys far greater flexibility in the long run. Indeed, the efficiency with which the user can manipulate files using DOS utility functions is directly related to how well the naming conventions are structured.

Another disadvantage is that codes used in elaborate filenaming schemes may be difficult for first-time users to remember. If one has 15 different file types and subtypes, as in Example 6–1, users will need either a reference sheet or "on-line" prompts and help screens. The disadvantages, however, probably seem minimal to anyone who has experienced the frustration of searching for a specific file among forty or more files that are all named "nancy," "nancy1," "testfile," and so on.

A final disadvantage is the close similarity between filenames; confusion can lead to the inadvertent erasure of data. For example, if a filename, FUD01084, is accidentally saved as FUD02084, the original FUD02084 file is lost; in addition, the new file (FUD01084) is misnamed as FUD02084. One must be very careful when saving, copying, or erasing files of similar names. Such hazards of using filenaming conventions underscore the necessity of regularly backing up your hard disk system.

6.4. A Summary of Useful Information on Filenaming Conventions

1. Filenaming conventions are best established at the time the machine is first installed. An agreed-upon set of rules for using filenames to identify and describe the contents of files allows multiple users to maintain a well-organized system.
2. Filenaming schemes can be designed around the use of column positions to describe up to eight attributes of a given file.
3. Filenaming schemes can be designed around short, meaningful syllables within the filename. As mnemonics, they may be easier to work with than column positions.

4. The same logic that is used in designing a filenaming convention scheme can be applied to the naming of directories and subdirectories.

5. Filenames within a naming scheme should all be a standard length. This permits the use of DOS's Global Filename Characters to more efficiently perform commands on a number of related files.

6. Filenaming conventions are not without their disadvantages: they require considerable upfront planning; the rules may become too complex and hard to remember; and operations on similarly named files must be performed with caution.

7.

Creating Batch Files

A *batch file* is a special file containing one or more commands that can be executed by DOS. When a batch file is activated, each command in the file is automatically executed. The effect is the same as it would be if each of the commands were issued sequentially by the user. A batch file is activated by entering the filename of the batch file as a command.

Batch files can be extremely useful. They allow the user to create his or her own customized DOS command sequences. For example, a series of interrelated DOS commands can be combined into a single batch file. The batch file then can be executed as if it were a command itself. Or, consider commands such as PATH and COPY. These commands often have many complicated parameters. Executing commands such as these can be greatly simplified when they are contained in a batch file. Batch files also can be helpful to inexperienced users. Standard procedures that involve running programs or accessing data can be simplified by batch routines.

Batch files vary in complexity and type. They may contain the usual DOS commands, or they may use a special set of commands found only in batch files. Some of these special batch commands have decision-making capabilities. Batch routines can be developed that use sophisticated, higher-level programming techniques. These special batch file commands are discussed in the next chapter.

This chapter is concerned with creating batch files. There are two ways to write a batch file in DOS. One may use either the COPY command or the DOS text-editing program, EDLIN. Each method has its own advantages and disadvantages. This chapter describes the two methods, and how batch files are used and modified. However, batch files do not have to be created in DOS to be used by DOS. Near the end of this chapter, there is a brief discussion of the alternatives available.

7.1. Creating a Batch File with the Copy Command

DOS allows the user to treat input from the keyboard as if it were input from a file. DOS reads the contents of a disk file as a series of characters. DOS can be fooled into believing that a series of characters coming from the keyboard is actually coming from a disk file. This is the basis for creating batch files with the COPY command. Data are copied from one "file" (the keyboard) to a new file, the batch file.

The Format of the Command

When the COPY command is used to create a batch file, it uses the format:

```
COPY CON: filename
```

The elements of this command have the following meaning:

> **CON:** This portion of the command specifies a reserved device name in DOS. CON stands for console. It actually has two meanings: When it designates an input device in a command, it represents the keyboard; when it designates an output device in a command, it represents the video screen. CON represents the keyboard in the above command.
>
> **filename** This is the name of the batch file being created. Any filename may be chosen that conforms to the normal rules of naming files. However, the filename MUST have .BAT as the filename extension. Also, the filename should not be the same as any DOS internal or external command.

Writing Batch Files with COPY CON:

When the COPY CON: command is issued, each text line entered at the keyboard is incorporated into the batch file. When the batch file is complete, an end-of-file marker (^Z) must be entered as the last line of the batch file. This is done by pressing the [F6] key and then the [Enter] key. The end-of-file marker also can be specified by holding down the [Ctrl] key and pressing the Z key; this also is followed by an [Enter].

The following example demonstrates a step-by-step approach to creating a simple batch file.

Example 7–1.

A batch file is created that automatically formats a floppy diskette, copies some files from the fixed disk to the newly formatted floppy, and then displays the contents of the floppy. This batch file is called FLOPCOPY.BAT. The default drive is C, and the current directory is the root directory. The procedure begins by entering the following command:

```
copy con: flopcopy.bat
```

The user then types the following command lines:

```
format a:
copy c:\sheet\*.wks a:
dir a:
^Z
```

The last line is the end-of-file marker; it is generated by pressing the [F6] function key. This ^Z ends the COPY CON: routine, completing the batch file.

Before a newly created batch file is activated, it is advisable to review the contents of the batch file. This is done to make sure that it contains all the desired commands, and that they have been typed correctly. The contents of batch files can be viewed with the TYPE command, which has the following format:

```
TYPE [d:][path][filename][.ext]
```

TYPE will display only text files; program files will appear in unreadable format. Global filename characters cannot be used. The contents can be printed by adding the ">PRN" symbols to the end of the command, or by pressing [Ctrl][PrtSc] before the command is entered. The [Crtl][Num Lock] keys can be used to halt temporarily the scrolling of a large file that is being displayed. The batch file in Example 7–1 is displayed on the screen with the following command:

```
type flopcopy.bat
```

The drive and path are not included in the above command, so the current directory and the default drive are assumed. Note that the display of the batch file does NOT show the end-of-file marker (^Z).

Making Changes and Correcting Mistakes

If the file contains errors, the user has two choices: 1) The entire batch file can be rewritten, starting over with the COPY CON: command from the beginning, or 2) the line or lines with the errors can be edited with the DOS text-editing program, EDLIN (use of the EDLIN program for making changes in batch files is discussed in section 7.3 of this chapter). These are the only two ways to correct errors or make changes in a batch file in DOS. If the batch file is fairly short, it is often easier to simply rewrite it from scratch with COPY CON:. For longer, more complex batch routines, using EDLIN is the more logical solution.

Activating the Batch File

To execute the commands in the newly-created FLOPCOPY.BAT file, it is necessary to enter only the filename of the batch file. Thus, the FLOPCOPY.BAT file can be executed by entering the following filename after the C> prompt:

`flopcopy`

Do not include the .BAT filename extension. When "FLOPCOPY" is entered, DOS processes each line of the FLOPCOPY batch file as if the FORMAT, COPY, and DIR commands had been entered individually by the user. The FORMAT command pauses and prompts the user to insert a diskette in drive A.

Figure 7–1 shows the screen output that might be generated when this batch file is executed.

Note: With DOS 3.X, the parameters [d:][path] may be placed in front of the batch filename. Batch files are like DOS external commands. That is, they reside on disk in a directory. These parameters allow the user to specify the particular drive and directory in which the command file is located. The pathname is separated from the command by a backslash (\).

```
        flopcopy

        C>format a:
        Insert new diskette for drive A:
        and strike any key when ready

        Formatting...Format complete

           362496 bytes total disk space
           362496 bytes available on disk

        Format another (Y/N)?n
        C>copy c:\sheet\*.wks a:
        C:\SHEET\BUDGET1.WKS
        C:\SHEET\FEEPROG.WKS
        C:\SHEET\REPRT.WKS
                3 File(s) copied

        C>dir a:

         Volume in drive A has no label
         Directory of  A:\

        BUDGET1    WKS      1620    1-01-80   12:02a
        FEEPROG    WKS      1834    1-01-80   12:02a
        REPRT      WKS      1989    1-01-80   12:03a
                3 File(s)      356352 bytes free

        C>
```

Figure 7–1. Screen information generated when the batch file FLOPCOPY.BAT is executed.

Batch Files and Interactive Prompts

A batch file may be written so that that the user must intervene. For example, to use the FORMAT command, the user must insert a diskette and "strike a key when ready." Or, interactive DOS commands can be written into the batch file command sequence. Although the computer can't reach out and insert its own diskette, the batch file can automatically respond to the "strike a key when ready" prompt. This is accomplished with the command line:

```
echo x ¦ format a:
```

where "x" represents the letter X key (any key can be used). The ¦ symbol indicates that a DOS pipe is in use. In this example, the pipe connects the display output of the ECHO command ("x" or any key) to the FORMAT command entered at the keyboard. Thus, if the unformatted diskette is already in Drive A, this command instructs DOS to look for the answer to the prompt when it executes the FORMAT command. This same technique can be used with any command in a batch file that requires an interactive prompt.

Halting a Batch File

Sometimes it may be necessary to interrupt the execution of batch file commands. For example, suppose a user inadvertently enters the name of the wrong batch file. The execution of a batch file can be halted by holding down the [Ctrl] key and pressing the [Break] key. DOS then pauses and displays the following message:

```
Terminate batch job (Y/N)?
```

Entering a Y (for "Yes") ends the batch file. Entering an N causes the batch file to resume from the next line FOLLOWING the interrupted line.

What Can Be Placed in Batch Files

The advantage of batch files such as FLOPCOPY.BAT is that they make the execution of frequently performed tasks faster and easier. In that sense, they may be thought of as user-customized DOS commands.

Any valid DOS command that can be typed at the keyboard may be placed in a batch file. However, the user must be aware of the internal and external nature of various DOS commands when using them in batch files. External DOS commands are not loaded into RAM with COMMAND.COM. Thus, if an external DOS command does not reside in the same directory with the batch file, some provision must be made for DOS to access the command. This might take the form of a PATH or a CD command in the batch file. Otherwise, the external DOS command in the batch files will not be executed. (It should be noted that DOS 3.X allows drive and path specifications to precede external DOS commands.)

Example 7–2.

FORMAT is an external DOS command. Assume that it resides in the root directory. If the batch file FLOPCOPY is located in another directory (e.g., UTILITY), the batch file routine will not work. This can be corrected by adding the CD\ command to the beginning of the batch file:

```
cd\

format a:

copy c:\sheet\*.wks a:

dir a:
```

If the batch file is being run under DOS 3.X, this problem also could be corrected by writing the FORMAT command with a pathname preceding it. This would make the CD command unnecessary:

```
\format a:

copy c:\sheet\*.wks a:

dir a:
```

Batch files also may contain non-DOS program names that nevertheless can be understood by DOS. Included in this category are program-activating commmands such as BASICA, LOTUS, or DBASE. These commands activate programs that run under the DOS operating system. If the PATH command has not been used, then the program must reside in the same directory as the batch file.

Finally, batch files may contain the names of other batch files. When the name of another batch file is encountered in the execution of batch file commands, command execution continues in the new batch file. It is this feature that allows the user to construct interesting and sophisticated DOS routines such as user-designed menus, password systems, and interactive programs.

The Advantages and Disadvantages of COPY CON: and EDLIN

The main advantage of creating batch files with the COPY CON: method is that it is a fairly quick and direct way to create short batch files. The COPY command is an internal DOS command. It is loaded into the computer's RAM memory when the system is started. This means that COPY CON: can be executed anywhere in the DOS directory hierarchy. EDLIN, on the other hand, is an external DOS program. It is stored on the fixed disk and/or the DOS diskette. To use EDLIN, the current directory must be the same directory where EDLIN resides, or the PATH command must be used. (DOS 3.X allows a drive and pathname to precede the EDLIN command.)

The principal disadvantage of the COPY CON: method of creating batch files is that there is no way to make changes or corrections in a line of the file after the line has been entered. Even if the F6 function key or the [Ctrl] and Z keys have not been pressed, there is no way to back up to a previous line once it has been entered. The user's only recourse is to end the COPY CON:

routine (by pressing either [F6], [Ctrl]-Z, [Ctrl] [Break], or [Ctrl]-C) and start over or to use EDLIN. The only way to edit an existing batch file in DOS is with EDLIN.

7.2. Creating Batch Files with EDLIN

EDLIN is the DOS text-editing program. It can be used to create, change, or display text files. The text of files created or edited in EDLIN is displayed in numbered lines. Each line may be up to 253 characters wide. Line numbers appear with each line of text, but the numbers are not stored with the file.

The EDLIN program is started by entering the EDLIN command and the filename of the new or existing file. The EDLIN command is entered in the following format:

`EDLIN [d:][path]filename[/B]`

The parameters have the following meaning:

d: This specifies the drive of the disk that is to contain the new file or the drive of the disk containing the existing file.

path The location of the file in the directory hierarchy is specified by this parameter.

filename This specifies the name of a new or an existing file. Batch files must have the .BAT extension.

/B When this parameter is included in the command, any ^Z characters (end-of-file markers) that are embedded in an existing file are ignored, and the entire file is loaded.

Note: With DOS 3.X, the parameter [d:][path] may be placed in front of the command. Since EDLIN is an external command, this allows the user to specify the particular drive and directory in which the command file is located. The pathname is separated from the command by a backslash (\).

The path, drive, and /B parameters are optional. However, a filename must always be specified. If this is not included, DOS displays the following error message:

`File name must be specified`

If the drive and path parameters are omitted, DOS looks for an existing file or places the new file in the current directory of the default drive. The /B parameter is only necessary if an existing file is known to contain embedded end-of-file markers.

The EDLIN system prompt for both new and existing files is the asterisk (*). Another characteristic of EDLIN is that its commands are activated by entering the first letter of the command name (e.g., the letter "I" is entered for Insert).

Creating a New Batch File with EDLIN

To create a new batch file with EDLIN, the EDLIN command is entered followed by the filename of the new batch file. For example, to create the FLOPCOPY.BAT file described in the previous section, the following command is entered:

```
edlin flopcopy.bat
```

Upper- or lower-case letters may be used. The filename MUST include the .BAT extension. Since the drive and path parameters have not been specified in the above command, the new batch file is placed in the current directory of the default drive. After the above command is entered, the following information is displayed:

```
New file

*
```

The asterisk is the EDLIN system prompt. It shows that EDLIN is ready to begin accepting the EDLIN commands.

The Insert and End Edit Commands

To begin building the new batch file, the EDLIN Insert command is used. This is done by entering the letter "I" after the system prompt. This causes the new file's first line number (1:) to be displayed. Figure 7–2 shows the screen display for these responses up to this point in the operation.

```
        C>edlin flopcopy.bat
        New file
        *i
             1:*
```

Figure 7–2. Creating a batch file using EDLIN. This is the screen display when the Insert command has been entered.

The user then types the first line or command of the batch file. When this is entered, EDLIN automatically displays the second line number. Each line of the batch file is typed and entered in this manner. After the last line has been entered, the Insert mode is terminated by holding down the [Ctrl] key and pressing [Break]. This enters ^C symbols as the last numbered line in the screen display. EDLIN responds with the * prompt. The user then must exit out of the EDLIN program by entering the EDLIN End Edit command. This is done by entering an E at the system prompt (the asterisk). The new batch file is now complete. Figure 7–3 shows the information that is displayed on the screen when the FLOPCOPY.BAT file is created.

```
C>edlin flopcopy.bat
New file
*i
        1:*format a:
        2:*copy c:\sheet\*.wks a:
        3:*dir a:
        4:*^Z
*e

C>
```

Figure 7–3. Screen display upon completion of FLOPCOPY.BAT batch file.

The Edit Line Command

The Edit Line command can be particularly useful when writing new batch files with EDLIN. It is most helpful when a batch file contains many lines or commands with multiple parameters. As mentioned above, one of the disadvantages of using the COPY CON: method to create batch files is that a line, once entered, cannot be edited. This is not the case in EDLIN. For example, suppose the second line of the above FLOPCOPY file is entered as

```
copy c:\sheet\*.wks
```

instead of

```
copy c:\sheet\*.wks a:
```

If the above error is discovered before the EDLIN session is terminated (i.e., before the "e" for the End Edit command has been entered), it may be corrected with the Edit Line command. However, if still in the Insert mode, the user first exits from the Insert mode by pressing the [Ctrl] and [Break] keys.

The Edit Line command is invoked by entering the line number to be edited.

─────────────────────────────*Example 7–3.*─────────────────────────

Suppose that line 2 contained the error described above. It can be corrected by entering the number 2 after the EDLIN system prompt:

```
    1: format a:

    2: copy c:\sheet\*.wks

    3: dir a:

    4: ^C
*2

    2: copy c:\sheet\*.wks

    2:*
```

The first line in the Edit mode redisplays the original (erroneous) second line of the file as it was entered. The cursor is positioned under this line after the second 2:. The user then types the replacement line and presses the [Enter] key. This ends the Edit Line command. In this example, a shortcut for retyping the entire line is the [F3] function key. When this key is pressed, it duplicates the original line; the new characters may then be added to the end of the line.

The [Esc] key or the [Ctrl] [Break] keys may be used to cancel the Edit Line mode without changing the original line in the file.

7.3. Editing an Existing Batch File

On many occasions, it may be necessary to add, delete, or change one or more lines in a batch file. The EDLIN program allows the user to change the contents of a batch file without completely rewriting it. One always has the option of rewriting the batch file from scratch using the COPY CON: routine. However, if the batch file has more than two or three lines, it is probably more convenient to use EDLIN.

There are a number of standard text-editing commands in EDLIN. There are commands that copy, move, and append lines of text in a batch file. EDLIN also is capable of performing search and replace routines. For the average user, however, these are not the most frequently used commands. This section covers in detail only those commands that are typically used in editing batch files. A summary of EDLIN's commands, command format, and explanations for each command is presented in Appendix C. Individuals interested in extensive text editing with EDLIN should refer to the DOS User's Manual for detailed discussions of the commands not covered here.

The Basic Commands

The commands discussed in this section allow the user to add, delete, display, and modify one or more lines in a batch file. The same format is used to activate the EDLIN program for new and existing batch files

```
EDLIN [d:][path]filename[/B]
```

Note that both the filename and the filename extension must be included. For an existing file, the following information is displayed on the screen when the command is entered:

```
End of input file

*
```

This means that the entire file has been loaded into the computer's memory, and that the user may proceed with the editing.

To edit lines in an existing batch file, a number of different EDLIN commands are used. With the exception of the Edit Line command, all of these commands are executed by entering the first letter of the command name. Also, it should be noted that a number of these commands involve the concept of the "current line." This is the line location in the file of the most recent change. It is marked by an asterisk (*) between the line number and the first character in the line. Aside from this, the asterisk should be completely ignored.

Editing a Line

To change a line in a batch file, the EDLIN Edit Line command is used. As described above (in **Creating Batch Files**), it is invoked by entering the line number of the line to be edited. This command is used in the same way for both an existing batch file and a new batch file.

Displaying the Lines of a Batch File

Once in the EDLIN program, it is often useful to have the numbered lines of a batch file displayed on the screen. This often makes it easier to perform various editing tasks. In EDLIN, the List Lines command will display up to 23 lines of a batch file. If the batch file is less than the 23-line maximum, the entire file may be displayed if the current line is line #1.

The user also may specify a range of lines to be displayed. This is done by entering the command in the following format:

```
[line][,line]L
```

The [line] parameters represent numbered lines in the batch file. For example, to display lines 6 through 10 of a batch file, the List Lines command would be entered as

```
6,10L
```

Note that a comma separates the two line numbers. If the line numbers are omitted (i.e., only the letter L is entered), up to 23 lines are displayed: 11 lines before the current line, the current line, and 11 lines after the current line. If the second line number is omitted (e.g., 6,L or 6L), then up to 23 lines are displayed, beginning with the specified line number.

For short batch files, it is convenient to display the entire file. If the first line is not the current line, this can be circumvented by entering the command as:

```
1L
```

In the FLOPCOPY.BAT file, this produces the following display:

```
*1L

    1:*format a:

    2: copy c:\sheet\*.wks a:

    3: dir a:
```

One can also use the Page (P) command to display the contents of a file. The Page command is entered in the same format as the List (L) command:

```
[line][,line]P
```

It permits the user to page through a file; 23 lines are displayed per "page." Unlike the List command, the P command changes the current line.

It should be remembered that it is not necessary to be in the EDLIN program to display the contents of a batch file. The TYPE command can be used for this purpose. However, TYPE does not display line numbers.

Adding Lines to a Batch File

New lines are added to an existing batch file with the EDLIN Insert Lines command. This command is entered in the following format:

```
[line]i
```

The [line] parameter is a numbered line in the batch file. The new line of text is inserted immediately BEFORE the specified line number. If no line number is specified, the new line is placed in the text before the current line. The line numbering is adjusted for the lines following the inserted line to reflect their new order.

After the first line is inserted, EDLIN allows the user to continue adding more lines by automatically displaying successive line numbers each time the [Enter] key is pressed. The Insert mode is terminated by holding down the [Ctrl] key and pressing either the [Break] key or the letter C.

To demonstrate the procedure for using the Insert Lines command, the previously discussed FLOPCOPY batch file will be used.

Example 7–4.

Suppose a user wished to insert the following line into this file:

```
copy c:\sheet\*.pic a:
```

The best way to determine where a new line should be placed in a batch file is to activate the EDLIN program and list the lines in the file. The screen display for these commands is shown below:

```
C>edlin flopcopy.bat

End of input file

*1L

    1:*format a:

    2: copy c:\sheet\*.wks

    3: dir a:

*
```

To insert the new line before line 3, the following command is entered:

```
3i
```

EDLIN responds to this command by displaying the line number and the system prompt:

```
3:*
```

After the user types the new third line and presses the [Enter] key, EDLIN displays the characters 4:* on the next line. This allows the user to add as many additional lines as needed in this location of the batch file. If no additional lines are needed, the Insert mode is terminated by holding down the [Ctrl] key and pressing either [Break] or the C key.

Before ending the EDLIN session, it is a good idea to use the List Lines command again to make sure that the new line or lines are positioned correctly in the file. After this is done, the EDLIN session is ended by entering the End Edit command. The screen display for this entire procedure is shown in Figure 7.4.

```
C>edlin flopcopy.bat
End of input file
*1L
        1:*format a:
        2: copy c:\sheet\*.wks a:
        3: dir a:
*3i
        3:*copy c:\sheet\*.pic a:
        4:*^C

*1L
        1: format a:
        2: copy c:\sheet\*.wks a:
        3: copy c:\sheet\*.pic a:
        4:*dir a:
*e

C>
```

Figure 7–4. Editing an existing batch file using the EDLIN Insert and List Lines commands.

Deleting Lines

The EDLIN Delete Lines command may be used to eliminate one or more lines from a batch file. This command has the following format:

```
[line][,line]d
```

To delete one specific line—for example, the third line—of a batch file, the command is entered as 3d or 3,d. To delete a range of lines, the first and last line numbers in the range must be specified. For example, to delete lines 2 through 5 in a batch file, the command is entered as:

```
2,5d
```

The comma separates the two line numbers. If no line numbers are specified, the current line is deleted.

In all cases, the remaining lines are renumbered.

The Transfer Lines Command

This command is used to merge the contents of another batch file into the batch file currently being edited. It is useful for adding standard command sequences that are frequently used in batch routines. These sequences can be entered into a batch file without being retyped. This command uses the following format:

```
[line]T[d:]filename
```

The [line] parameter is a numbered line in the current batch file. The contents of the specified file are inserted ahead of the line number; if this is omitted, then the contents are inserted ahead of the current line. "T" stands for the Transfer command. The [d:] parameter is the drive of the disk that contains the file being combined with the current batch file.

For example, to combine the contents of a file called DUPE.BAT with a file currently being edited, the following command would insert the lines of that file starting at line 3:

```
3tdupe.bat
```

EDLIN searches for the DUPE.BAT file in the current directory of the default drive.

The End Edit and Quit Commands

The EDLIN program can be ended in two different ways. The End Edit command ends the current EDLIN session and saves the batch file under the filename specified at the start of EDLIN. Additionally, when editing an existing .BAT file, the original batch file is renamed with a .BAK filename extension. This means that the original file is automatically preserved as a backup. The End Edit command is processed by entering the letter E at the EDLIN system prompt.

The Quit command allows the user to exit the EDLIN program without saving any changes that have been made in the file during the current editing session. This command is activated by entering the letter Q at the EDLIN system prompt. In addition, the original file is not renamed with the .BAK extension. When the command is entered, the following message is displayed:

```
Abort edit (Y/N)?
```

Entering a "Y" ends the EDLIN session. Entering an "N" or any other character continues the current EDLIN session. This prevents the user from inadvertently exiting the program without saving any changes made to the file.

7.4. Creating Batch Files outside of DOS

Batch files may be created outside of DOS in any program that is capable of storing data in a ASCII format. The ASCII (American Standard Code for Information Interchange) format is a standard method of storing English letters, numbers, and characters. Most text editing programs and word processors can generate this type of file.

Note that word processing programs such as MultiMate and WordStar normally store data in document files (.DOC extensions). This is not a text format. A document file must be converted to a text format before it can be read as a batch file.

Using non-DOS sources to create batch files can be more convenient than using EDLIN or COPY CON:. This is particularly true when writing or editing batch routines of any length. However, there is a small trade-off: Once a batch file has be written and edited, the user must shift into DOS to try out the new batch file. This may involve some inconvenience, depending on how easy it is to get from the text editing program to DOS.

7.5. Some Rules and Suggestions for Writing and Using Batch Files

1. The root portion of batch filenames may be one to eight characters in length. All the usual rules for naming files must be followed.
2. All batch files MUST have .BAT as the filename extension.
3. The filename for a batch file cannot be the same as any DOS command such as COPY or ERASE.
4. Batch files cannot be given filenames that are the same as program filenames that reside in the same directory as the batch file. Program filenames have extensions of .EXE or .COM.
5. Any valid DOS command that can be typed at the keyboard can be placed in a batch file. Also, the names of other batch files may be entered in a batch file. When another batch filename is encountered during the execution of batch commands, DOS shifts to the new batch file and begins executing those commands.
6. If a user wishes to edit or change a batch file by using the COPY CON: method of writing batch files, the entire batch file must be rewritten from the beginning. DOS writes over the old version with the new one.
7. In DOS 2.X, only batch files residing in the current directory can be executed unless the PATH command is used. This command specifies alternate directories to be searched for programs and batch files not found in the current directory. In DOS 3.X, a drive and pathname

may be used in front of the batch filename to direct DOS to the location of the batch file.

8. It is not necessary to enter the .BAT portion of a batch filename to execute a batch file. Only the root portion of the filename is necessary.

9. Interactive pauses generated by DOS commands (i.e., Y/N prompts) operate as usual in a batch file. The user may either respond to these prompts or the response can be built into the batch file using the ECHO command and DOS's piping features.

10. Batch file execution may be halted by holding down the [Ctrl] key and pressing either the [Break] or C keys. There may be a delay until these commands are recognized.

11. DOS 3.X allows a portion of the computer's memory to be used to simulate an additional disk drive while the computer is turned on. This is called a RAM disk, and batch files that are copied onto this temporary storage device are executed at considerably faster speeds than from the mechanical disk drives. A RAM disk is created in DOS 3.X through the use of the VDISK command. This command is placed in the CONFIG.SYS file. See Chapter 9 for a discussion of the CONFIG.SYS file, and how it is created and used.

8.

More on Batch Files

Batch files vary in versatility, complexity, and type. As seen in the previous chapter, a batch file may contain the usual DOS commands such as COPY, FORMAT, and DIR. However, there is another set of DOS commands that is used only in batch files. These commands allow the user to construct batch routines of much greater versatility and sophistication. Some of these commands may be used to perform decision-making routines.

Another means for creating versatile batch files is though a special method of specifying DOS command parameters in batch files. Parameters are those extra, variable specifications that are included on the command line with DOS commands such as COPY. Batch routines can be written that permit substitution of different parameters in the batch file commands each time the batch routine is run.

These topics and other relevant subjects are covered in this chapter. Near the end of the chapter are some sample batch routines and explanations of how they work. The final section presents a summary of some of the basic rules that must be followed for creating and using these files.

8.1. Using Replaceable Parameters

When batch file commands require parameters such as filenames, drive specifications, paths, and so on, one or more of the parameters may be given a special notation. This notation indicates that these parameters are specified by the user each time the batch file is executed. This means that the user may input different parameters for those commands every time the batch file is run, without having to change the contents of the file. When parameters in batch file commands are written in this manner, they are called *Replaceable Parameters* or *Batch File Variables*.

How to Specify Replaceable Parameters

To understand how replaceable parameters are used in a batch file, consider the following example:

—————————————— **Example 8–1.** ——————————————

A batch file is needed that allows a user to create a backup copy of a new file on a floppy diskette. The files always have the same filename extension; however, each filename may be different every time the batch routine is executed. The user also would like to use the DIR command to verify that the new file has been copied onto the diskette. The batch file that would be written for this situation is as follows:

```
copy c:%1.wrk a:

dir a:%1.wrk
```

In the above example, the symbols %1 represent the replaceable filename parameter. When this batch file is executed, the user must specify the filename that is to be substituted for the %1 symbols in the batch file commands COPY and DIR. Suppose the above batch file is called BACKCOPY.BAT. To have the batch file perform its copying routine on a file called BUDGET.WRK, the following command is entered:

```
backcopy budget
```

Notice that the .WRK filename extension is not included because this is already specified in the batch file. This command would produce the following screen display:

```
C>COPY C:BUDGET.WRK A:

        1 File(s) copied

C>DIR A:BUDGET.WRK


Volume in drive A has no label

Directory of  A:\


BUDGET   WRK      1543  1-01-80     1:33a

     1 File(s)      13312 bytes free
```

The same batch file could be used to copy many different files. For example, to have the BACKCOPY batch file copy a file called TRAVEL.WRK, the following command is entered:

```
backcopy travel
```

In each case, the filenames BUDGET and TRAVEL are substituted for the %1 replaceable parameter in the batch file.

Using More Than One Replaceable Parameter

Up to ten different replaceable parameters may be specified in a batch file. All replaceable parameters begin with the percent sign (%), followed by a number from 0 to 9. The replaceable parameter %0 is reserved for designating the name of the batch file itself in the batch file, if this is necessary. It may not be used for any other purpose. The numbering for all other valid command parameters begins with %1. To demonstrate how several different parameters are used in a batch file, consider the next example:

───────────────────── *Example 8–2.* ─────────────────────

A user wishes to modify the original BACKCOPY batch file described in Example 8–1 so that it copies a file to the floppy disk drive under a different filename. The filename extension remains the same for the duplicate. Again, the user would like to verify that the new file has been copied, using the DIR command. The new batch file for this situation would be written in the following way:

```
copy c:%1.wrk a:%2.wrk

dir a:%2.wrk
```

Notice that two different replaceable parameters are now specified with the symbols %1 and %2. The %2 that is used with the DIR command represents the same filename as the %2 in the COPY command, so it is simply repeated. Since the drive and filename extension still do not change, replaceable parameters are needed only for the two different filenames. With this batch file, any file with the .WRK filename extension located on the fixed disk can be copied to a floppy under a new name. For example, suppose a user wishes to copy a file called BUDGET.WRK to a floppy diskette as BUDGET2.WRK. If the batch file again is called BACKCOPY.BAT, the command that would perform this operation is:

```
backcopy budget budget2
```

Notice that spaces separate the batch filename BACKCOPY and the two command parameters. (Commas could be used as well.) Figure 8–1 illustrates where the parameters included on the command line are substituted into the batch file. The first parameter (BUDGET) is substituted for the %1 replaceable parameter in the batch file; the second parameter entered on the command line (BUDGET2) is substituted for the %2 replaceable parameter in the batch file. The COPY and DIR commands are processed as if they were written in the batch file as:

```
copy c:budget.wrk a:budget2.wrk

dir a:budget2.wrk
```

Figure 8–2 shows the screen display that is produced by executing this batch routine.

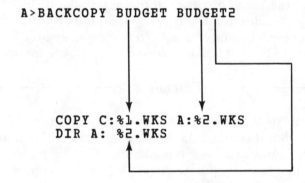

Figure 8–1. Replacing dummy parameters with batch command line parameters. The second parameter (BUDGET2) is used in two locations in the batch file.

```
C>backcopy budget budget2

C>copy c:budget.wks a:budget2.wks
        1 File(s) copied

C>dir a:budget2.wks

 Volume in drive A has no label
 Directory of  A:\

BUDGET2  WKS     3483    1-01-80    1:00a
        1 File(s)    344064 bytes free

C>
```

Figure 8–2. Screen display generated by the BACKCOPY.BAT batch file.

The BACKCOPY batch file can be made even more versatile with the use of a third replaceable parameter:

```
copy c:%1.wrk %2%3.wrk

dir %2%3.wrk
```

Now the %2 replaceable parameter can be used to specify either a different drive or a directory path. That is, the same batch file could be used to copy a .WRK file to either a floppy disk or a specified subdirectory on the fixed disk. For example, the command

```
backcopy budget  a:  budget2
```

copies the BUDGET.WRK file onto a floppy diskette under the filename BUDGET2.WRK. Observe how spaces are used to separate the second parameter (a:) from the other two. Commas could be used instead of spaces.

Omitting Replaceable Parameters

In a batch file with replaceable parameters, the user does not necessarily have to specify all the parameters when the batch routine is executed. For example, consider another batch file with three replaceable parameters:

```
copy c:%1 %2%3

dir %2%3
```

The first replaceable parameter (%1) can be used to specify the source file for the COPY command. The second replaceable parameter (%2) may specify either another drive or a directory path for the target file of the COPY command. The third replaceable parameter may specify the new filename for the target file. Suppose this batch file is called DUPE.BAT. The command

```
dupe travel.doc,\wp\,travel2.doc
```

will copy the file TRAVEL.DOC into the WP subdirectory under the new filename of TRAVEL2.DOC. Note that commas separate the directory parameter from the two other parameters. The screen display generated by the above command is shown in Figure 8–3.

Now, suppose the last parameter is omitted, as in

```
dupe travel.doc,a:
```

Here, the replaceable parameter (%2) specifies the drive instead of the directory path. The third replaceable parameter (%3) is not specified on the command line. Thus, the TRAVEL.DOC file is copied to the floppy disk under the same filename, and the DIR command in the batch file produces a listing of all the files on the floppy. DOS simply ignores the %3 parameter in the batch file.

```
C>dupe travel.doc \wp\ travel2.doc

C>copy c:travel.doc \wp\travel2.doc
        1 File(s) copied

C> dir \wp\travel2.doc

 Volume in drive C is DPlus
 Directory of  C:\wp

 TRAVEL2  DOC      1223     1-08-84     12:03a
        1 Files(s)      7844335 bytes free

C>
```

Figure 8–3. Screen display produced by the DUPE.BAT batch file.

8.2. Special Batch File Commands

DOS has a number of commands that are used exclusively in batch files. These commands allow the user to construct batch routines of even greater versatility and sophistication. The commands are REM, ECHO, PAUSE, IF, GOTO, FOR, and SHIFT. These commands may be used ONLY in batch files. The CLS command is not restricted to batch files, but is particularly useful in batch routines. All of these commands are discussed below.

REM (Remark)

   This command allows the user to place descriptive commentary in the batch file. It can be used to make the contents and the purpose of the commands in a batch file more understandable. The command has the following format:

```
REM [remark]
```

The [remark] may consist of up to 123 letters, characters, numbers, or spaces. It is displayed on the screen along with the REM command itself during the execution of the batch file.

   To demonstrate how REM might be used, consider this short batch file:

_____*Example 8–3.*_____

```
rem  This batch file creates floppy backups for spread-
sheet files

copy c:*.wks a:

rem  Here is a list of the files on the floppy disk

dir a:
```

The two REM commands inform the user of what the batch file is doing. The remarks are displayed on the screen along with the rest of the information generated by the batch file. Figure 8–4 shows the screen output that might be produced by this batch file. (The file is called BACKCOPY.BAT.)

DOS 2.X also allows the period (.) to be substituted for the REM command (DOS 3.X, however, does not). In a batch file, a command line that begins with a period is interpreted to mean REM. This can be useful when the word REM may be otherwise confusing to the user.

```
C>rem  This batch file creates floppy backups for spreadsheet files

C>copy c:*.wks a:
C:JOURNAL.WKS
C:AUTO123.WKS
C:MEMO.WKS
C:RATE.WKS
        4 File(s) copied

C>rem  Here is a list of the files on the floppy disk

C>dir a:

 Volume in drive A has no label
 Directory of  A:\

JOURNAL  WKS    17152   4-12-84   8:38a
AUTO123  WKS     2432   5-28-84   7:40p
MEMO     WKS     5197   1-01-80   5:58a
RATE     WKS     1536   6-02-84   1:30p
        4 File(s)    333824 bytes free

C:>
```

Figure 8–4. Information displayed on the screen upon execution of the BACKCOPY.BAT file. The REM command is used to display the messages.

Echo

This batch file command allows the user to control the display of the command lines during the execution of the batch routine. It also can be used to display a message on the screen.

When ECHO is used to control the display of batch file commands on the screen, it has two different formats: ECHO ON or ECHO OFF. Normally, each line of a batch file is displayed on the screen as it is executed by DOS. That is, the ECHO ON command is automatically in effect. If the user does not wish to have the batch commands displayed as they are executed, the first command in the batch file should be ECHO OFF. The ECHO OFF command itself is displayed, but no other batch command after it will appear on the screen until an ECHO ON command is encountered. There is no need to end the batch file with ECHO ON, as DOS automatically returns to the ECHO ON mode when the batch routine ends. It is important to note that the ECHO OFF prevents only the batch file commands from being displayed on the screen; it has no effect on the display of information generated by the commands themselves. For example, a DIR command in a batch file will still show a listing of filenames on the screen, even if ECHO OFF is in effect.

─────────────── *Example 8–4.* ───────────────

The following batch files demonstrate the use of ECHO OFF and ECHO ON.

```
rem   Now is the time...

echo off

rem   ...for all good men...

copy c:budget.doc a:

echo on

rem   ...to come to the aid of their country.
```

The execution of this batch file generates the following screen display:

```
rem   Now is the time...

echo off

1 File(s) copied

rem   ...to come to the aid of their country.
```

Notice that the display of the second REM command is suppressed, and that the usual DOS response to a successful COPY command is displayed.

Sometimes a user may want to have a message displayed while the ECHO OFF command is in effect. This is done by using a different format for the ECHO command:

`ECHO [message]`

Only the message is displayed on the screen. This format of the ECHO command does not change the status of the ECHO OFF mode. The following batch file shows how it might be used:

──────────────── *Example 8–5.* ────────────────


```
echo off

echo This is a list of spreadsheet and word-processing
files

dir c:\123files

dir c:\wpfiles
```

When executed, the above batch file would generate the kind of screen display shown in Figure 8–5.

The ECHO command is particularly useful when the display of batch file commands might be confusing or distracting. Using ECHO OFF and ECHO ON with the ECHO [message] format allows the user to selectively control what batch file commands and messages appear on the screen.

```
C>display

C>echo off
This is a list of spreadsheet and word-processing files

 Volume in drive C is XTMGMT
 Directory of  C:\123files

        .           <DIR>       6-23-84    6:32p
        ..          <DIR>       6-23-84    6:32p
     JOURNAL  WKS    17152      4-12-84    8:38a
     AUTO123  WKS     2432      5-28-84    7:40p
            4 File(s)    7602176 bytes free

       Volume in drive C is XTMGMT
       Directory of  C:\wpfiles

        .           <DIR>       6-23-84    6:31p
        ..          <DIR>       6-23-84    6:31p
     CHAPTER1 DOC     1664      4-21-84    5:17p
     CHAPTER2 DOC    31232      6-03-84    7:51a
     CHAPTER3 DOC    23680      5-12-84    9:27a
            5 File(s)    7602176 bytes free

C>
```

**Figure 8–5. Screen display generated upon execution of the
BACKCOPY.BAT file. Note that ECHO OFF produces only the message,
unlike the REM command.**

PAUSE

This batch file command halts the execution of the batch file, displays an
optional message, and follows it with the prompt "Strike a key when
ready...." Execution of the batch file is resumed when a key is pressed.
PAUSE has the following format:

PAUSE [message]

The [message] parameter is optional. This command is useful for situations
when the user must perform some task before the batch routine can proceed.
Consider the following batch file:

─────────────────────── *Example 8–6.* ───────────────────────

echo off

cls

echo This batch file copies all the spreadsheet files.

```
echo Please make sure that the BACKUP diskette is in
drive A.

pause

copy c:\123files\*.* a:
```

The type of information displayed on the screen by this batch file is shown in Figure 8–6. If the PAUSE command is followed by a message, it may be up to 121 letters, numbers, characters, or spaces.

The execution the batch file can be aborted entirely during the pause by holding down the [Ctrl] key and pressing the [Break] key.

```
        This batch file copies all the spreadsheet files.
        Please make sure that the BACKUP diskette is in Drive A.
Strike any key when ready . . .
```

Figure 8–6. User-designed screen prompts generated by batch routine of Example 8–6.

CLS (Clear Screen)

This is not a command that is restricted to batch files. CLS can be used anywhere in DOS. However, it is particularly useful in batch routines as a way of controlling the screen display. When this command is entered, all information on the screen is cleared. The prompt or cursor then moves to the upper left-hand corner of the screen. For example, a batch file might display a message or call up a user-designed menu. The CLS command can be used to blank the screen just before the message or menu is displayed. The screen then contains only the desired information.

IF

This is a decision-making batch file command. It allows other batch commands to be executed only if a specified condition is true. If the condition is false, the command is ignored. The conditional portion of this command is the factor that makes the IF command so versatile. IF has the following format:

```
IF [NOT] [condition] [command]
```

The condition parameter may be expressed in one of three ways. Each is described below. Also included in the discussion is the [NOT] parameter.

The EXIST Condition

This condition tests for the existence of a specified file. When used with the IF command, its format is

```
IF EXIST [filespec] [command]
```

or

```
IF NOT EXIST [filespec] [command]
```

The filespec parameter is a filename and an optional filename extension. An optional drive specification may be included. Pathnames are not allowed. This condition performs a specified command only if a particular file exists when the batch file is executed. Conversely, when the NOT parameter is used, a specified command is performed only if a particular file does not exist. Here is an example of a batch file using IF with the EXIST condition:

─────────────────── *Example 8–7.* ───────────────────

```
echo off

if exist a:%1 echo File already on floppy. Hit [Ctrl][Break] to end.
Or,

pause

copy c:%1 a:
```

The above batch file is used to back up individual files to a floppy diskette. The %1 replaceable parameter allows this routine to be used for any file. If the file already exists on the floppy, the user is given the option of not over-writing it. If the file does not already exist on the floppy, the pause still occurs, but no ECHO message is displayed. Figure 8–7 shows the screen display when the EXIST condition is true and the operation is aborted. The batch file is called DUPE.BAT and the copied file is named BUDGET1.WKS.

```
C>dupe budget1.wks

C>echo off
File already on floppy. Press [Ctrl][Break] to end. Or
Strike a key when ready ... ^C

Terminate batch job (Y/N)? y
```

Figure 8–7. The DUPE.BAT file screen display. The files are not copied if the EXIST condition is true.

The string1 = = string2 Condition

This condition in the IF command tests whether one character string is equal to another character string. It has the following format when used with the IF command:

```
IF [string1==string2] [command]
```

Translated, this means "If the string entered by the user (string1) is equal to this specific string (string2), then do this command." Notice that two equal signs are used in the command. If the two strings match, character for character, then the condition is true and the command is performed. If the two strings do not match, then the command is ignored and the next line of the batch file is executed. The two strings also must be equivalent in their use of upper- and lower-case letters.

The batch file shown below demonstrates how this condition might be used with the IF command. Its function is to display different portions of the files in a directory system.

Example 8–8.

```
echo off

if %1==all dir c:\/w/p

if %1==text dir c:\wp\wpfiles/w/p

if %1==sheet dir c:\sheet\123files/w/p
```

The first line turns off the display of batch file commands. The string1 is a replaceable parameter (%1), so the user may enter any character string when the batch file is executed. For example, when the string "all" is entered with the batch filename, a listing of all root directory files is shown in a wide screen display, with a pause occurring each time the screen is filled. Similarly, the strings "text" and "sheet" generate displays of specific subdirectory filenames. Note that the string "Sheet" or "SHEET" would not produce any results because of the upper-case letters. This batch file is called DISPLAY. Figure 8–8 shows the information that might be generated when this batch file is executed, using "sheet" as the parameter.

```
C>display sheet

C>echo off

 Volume in drive C is DunsPlus
 Directory of  C:\sheet\123files

      .                  ..              OPUS2   WKS     OPUS2   PRN     DFPTEST1 WKS
    MODELWP PRN     BANKMOD1 WKS     ADMIN   WKS     TRAVEL  WKS     MEMO    WKS
    DATAEDIT WKS    BANKMOD4 WKS     MESSAGE1 PRN    MESSAGE2 PRN    UPDATE  WKS
    MEG     WKS     ADMIN4  WKS      RATE30  WKS     RATE60  WKS     RATE90  WKS
    RATE120 WKS     DATAEDIT PRN     QUEST   WKS     QUEST2  WKS     QUEST3  WKS
    MESSAGE3 PRN    DFP2    WKS      SOFT    WKS     MESSAGE4 PRN
       29 File(s)     4558848 bytes free

C>
```

Figure 8–8. The information that is generated by DISPLAY.BAT when it is executed using the "sheet" parameter.

The ERRORLEVEL Condition

This condition in the IF command can be used to test if specific DOS commands or programs have been completed successfully. The error code scheme currently is used by only two DOS commands, BACKUP and RESTORE.

Applications programs that use error code schemes typically set the error level at 0 if the program has been completed successfully. When such programs do not successfully complete their operations, the error level usually is set at different positive values, depending on the nature of the error. Typically, the seriousness of the error increases as the value of the error code increases. The user's manual accompanying the program should be consulted for the error-level code scheme used by that program, if any.

Since BACKUP and RESTORE are the only DOS commands using an error code scheme, the use of the ERRORLEVEL condition in the IF command is described in this context only. When either of these commands is issued, the error level may have one of four different values:

Error Level	Explanation
0	BACKUP or RESTORE successfully completed.
1	No files found to BACKUP or RESTORE.
3	User has aborted operation with [Ctrl] [Break].
4	Hardware or other type of error encountered.

Using the error codes shown above, the following batch file could be used to display a message after a successful backup of some specific files in a directory:

──────────────────── *Example 8–9.* ────────────────────

```
echo off

backup c:\sheet\123files\*.wks a:

if errorlevel 1 echo Problems: Backup terminated!!

if not errorlevel 1 echo Backup successful.
```

The ERRORLEVEL 1 condition tests for error codes of 1 *or greater*. Thus, the IF command will produce the "Problems" message if error codes 1, 3, or 4 are encountered. The use of the NOT parameter in the last command line allows the "Backup successful" message to be displayed only if error codes 1, 3, or 4 are not encountered.

GOTO

This is a very useful command for controlling the order of execution of batch file commands. It is similar in function to the GOTO commands of higher-level programming languages such as BASIC and PL/I. Descriptive labels in the batch file are used as location points for the GOTO command. A batch file LABEL begins with a colon (:) followed by any character string from one to eight characters long. Command execution can be shifted to any of these points with the GOTO command. The command has the following format:

```
GOTO [label]
```

Labels may be longer than eight characters, but DOS recognizes only the first eight. This command is particularly versatile when used in conjunction with the IF batch command.

The following example demonstrates how the GOTO command might be used in a batch file:

──────────────────── *Example 8–10.* ────────────────────

```
echo off

backup c:\sheet\123files\*.wks a:

if errorlevel 1 goto abort

echo Backup successful.

goto end
```

```
:abort

echo Problems... Backup terminated!!

:end
```

The batch file in Example 8–10 is similar to the batch file of Example 8–9, except that only one IF command is used to achieve the same effect. Notice that the labels used in the GOTO command do not include the colons. If the condition in the IF command is true (i.e., if the BACKUP command generates an error code of 1 or greater), then the command execution is shifted down to :abort. The label itself is ignored, and the "Problems" message is displayed. If the condition in the IF command is false, then the "Backup successful" message is displayed, and command execution is shifted to the :end label.

Labels in a batch file are never displayed when the file is executed. This means that they can be used throughout a batch file for descriptive purposes as an alternative to the REM command. (REM statements are displayed unless ECHO OFF is in effect.) If a GOTO command directs command execution to a label that does not exist in the batch file, the batch routine is ended and the following error message is displayed:

```
Label not found
```

FOR

The FOR batch file command allows the user to construct batch routines that perform a DOS command on each item in a list of files. FOR makes it possible to avoid entering the same command over and over for a series of different files. This command has the following format:

```
FOR %%variable IN (set) DO [command]
```

The parameters in this command have the following meaning:

variable   This is a single upper- or lower-case letter, and it represents a dummy filename. During the execution of the FOR command, the files specified in set (which is a list of filenames) are substituted sequentially for variable (the dummy filename).

set   This is the list of filenames to be the subject of the command. Each item in the list is separated by a space. File specifications may include the filename, the filename extension, and the drive specification. Pathnames are not allowed. Wild card characters (the * and ? symbols) may be used in filenames. Also, replaceable parameters can be used (e.g., %1, %2, and so on). The files must be in the current directory for drive C.

command   This is the action that is to be taken on each of the items in the set. It is any internal DOS command such as DIR, COPY, or DEL.

Note: Although pathnames are not allowed in the set parameter in DOS 2.X, they are permitted in DOS 3.X.

Notice in particular the syntax used in the FOR command. The variable parameter must be preceded by two percent signs (%%) and the filenames in the set parameter are enclosed in parentheses.

Suppose a user wants to print the contents of different batch files. The FOR command could be used in a small batch routine to accomplish this task:

```
echo off

for %%a in (dupe.bat backcopy.bat display.bat) do type %%a>prn
```

The %%a parameter represents the variable (the dummy filename). Any single letter could be used (e.g., %%b, %%x, and so on). Each filename in the set is substituted for this variable when the FOR command is executed. Notice that %%a is placed after "for" as well as before "type." When this batch file is executed, the contents of all three files specified in the set are printed. The ">prn" portion of the above command directs the output of the TYPE command to the printer. The FOR command in the above batch file has the same effect as when each of these commands is executed separately:

```
type dupe.bat>prn

type backcopy.bat>prn

type display.bat>prn
```

The files specified in the set may use global filename characters (wild cards). This is a useful way of processing many files in a set without typing every filename. For example, in the above batch file, all the batch files in the current directory could be printed by writing the FOR command as follows:

```
echo off

for %%a in (*.bat) do type %%a>prn
```

The set also can be left as a variable by specifying the set as a replaceable parameter, as in:

```
for %%a in (%1 %2 %3) do type %%a>prn
```

SHIFT

The purpose of the SHIFT batch file command is to increase the number of replaceable parameters that can be placed in a batch file (DOS normally allows a maximum of ten). As described previously, replaceable parameters begin with the percent sign (%) followed by a number from 0 to 9. The %0 parameter is used only to specify the name of the batch file itself.

If an occasion arises in which the user finds it necessary to place more than nine or ten different replaceable parameters in a batch file, the SHIFT command may prove helpful. It must be remembered that each replaceable parameter used in a batch file generally requires the user to enter the "real" parameter on the command line with the batch filename. Having to enter ten or more parameters to run a batch routine may prove to be something of a nuisance.

For more information on how the SHIFT command is used, the reader should refer to the batch file commands in the DOS User's Manual.

8.3. The AUTOEXEC.BAT File

DOS has a special facility for automatic execution of specific batch files. Whenever the computer is turned on or a system restart is performed (i.e., [Ctrl] [Alt] [Del]), DOS searches for a batch file named AUTOEXEC.BAT. If such a file exists, DOS automatically executes this file. The filename AUTOEXEC.BAT should be used only for a batch file that the user wants executed when the system is turned on or restarted.

The AUTOEXEC.BAT file must reside in the root directory of the disk that is used for the system startup. The XT and AT will read from a floppy disk drive (drive A) if there is a diskette in this drive and the drive door is closed. If this is not the case, the system will read from the fixed disk. Thus, the user has the option of placing AUTOEXEC.BAT files on floppy diskettes, high-capacity floppy diskettes, or the root directory of the fixed disk. The AUTOEXEC.BAT file on the fixed disk is ignored when a floppy drive is used for the startup.

AUTOEXEC.BAT files are created like any other batch file. Either the COPY CON: command or the EDLIN program may be used to create them. The only difference between this type of batch file and normal batch files is in the use of the AUTOEXEC.BAT filename.

This facility is useful in a number of different ways. For example, suppose the same command or the same set of commands is always executed when the computer is turned on. The user can have DOS execute these commands automatically by placing them in a batch file called AUTOEXEC.BAT. The AUTOEXEC.BAT file also can be a very valuable tool when the computer is operated by inexperienced users. The novice user can avoid having to enter commands such as DATE and TIME, or program names and search paths (the PATH command). Many applications programs have their own AUTOEXEC.BAT files that automatically start the program. In dBASE II, for example, the AUTOEXEC file consists of a single command: dbase. Lotus 1-2-3 has a simple batch file consisting of the following commands:

```
date

time

lotus
```

The first two commands are the DOS DATE and TIME commands; the third command activates the program and displays the Lotus Access System menu. AUTOEXEC.BAT files also can be used to display a user's customized DOS menu at the system startup.

A sample AUTOEXEC.BAT file is described in Section 8.5. The use of the AUTOEXEC.BAT file in user-designed menus is described in Chapter 9.

8.4. The PROMPT Command

The PROMPT command allows the user to control the appearance of the DOS system prompt. It is included in the discussion of batch files because it is most useful when utilized in this context. The standard DOS prompt can be converted into an informational prompt that tells the user the date, the time of day, or the current directory. Or, the prompt may simply display a directive, such as:

```
ENTER COMMAND>
```

The prompt command has the following format:

```
PROMPT [prompt-text]
```

The [prompt-text] is the text that is to be used for the new system prompt. For example, if the command

```
prompt ENTER COMMAND:
```

is entered, the new DOS system prompt is

```
ENTER COMMAND:
```

Special characters (metastrings) that display specific types of information can be used after the PROMPT command. All of these special characters are preceded by the $ character.

$	The $ character.
t	The time.
d	The date.
p	The current directory of the default drive.
v	The version number.
n	The default drive.
g	The > character.
l	The < character.
b	The ¦ character.
q	The = character.
_ (underscore)	A carriage return/linefeed sequence (go to the beginning of the next line on the display screen).

Here are some examples of prompts that are generated using the above characters:

Command	Prompt Displayed
prompt tg	11:02:31>
prompt ENTER COMMAND$g	ENTER COMMAND>
prompt dg	Tues 9-17-1985>

The system prompt is returned to normal by entering the PROMPT command with no arguments.

8.5. Some Useful Batch Files

This section describes some sample batch routines. The intention here is to show how sophisticated batch files can help the user in the general maintenance and management of the XT and AT.

Example: Performing a Text Search

Suppose a search must be performed through all of a system's text files for references to a particular company (Silicon MegaSystems). Using a batch file and the FIND filter, this task can be completely automated. FIND searches for all occurrences of a particular character string in each of the specified files. Although FIND does not permit the use of global filename characters, the FOR command can be used to get around this limitation. Also, using a replaceable parameter, the batch file can be used to search for any specified character string, not just "Silicon MegaSystems." The contents of this batch file are as follows:

```
echo off

path \utility

for %%f in (*.dat) do find /n"%1" %%f
```

Note that the FIND command can be used only on text (ASCII) files. Attempting to perform a FIND on binary files such as MultiMate and 1-2-3 will not work. The commands in the above batch file have the following meaning:

echo off   This turns off the display of batch file commands while the batch file is being executed.

path \utility   This command tells DOS to search in the UTILITY subdirectory for any batch file, command, or program not found in the current directory. This is needed in DOS 2.X because FIND is an external command. That is, it is not a command loaded into RAM memory with the DOS COMMAND.COM file. In this example, it is stored in a subdirectory called UTILITY. (In DOS 3.X, a drive and pathname can be specified in front of the FIND command to indicate to DOS the command's location.)

for %%f in (*.dat) do find /n"%1" %%f

The (*.dat) specification in the FOR command causes the FIND command to be performed on every file in the current directory having the .dat filename extension. The %%f functions as the dummy for each "real" file in the (*.dat) set. The "%1" represents the character string that is the subject of the search. Using a replaceable parameter here means that any string entered on the command line with the batch filename can be the subject of a search.

Suppose this batch routine is called SEARCH.BAT. To perform the search in the text files for the string "Silicon MegaSystems," the following command would be entered:

```
search Silicon MegaSystems
```

The string after the SEARCH filename replaces the %1 replaceable parameter in the batch file. The output that might be generated by this command is shown in Figure 8-9. (Note that the current directory must be the same directory containing the *.dat files if this batch file is run in DOS 2.X. In this version of DOS, FOR does not allow the use of pathnames; this is not the case in DOS 3.X.)

```
search Silicon MegaSystems

C>echo off

---------- ADDRESS.DAT

---------- DOC$IO.DAT

---------- DATAEDIT.DAT

---------- OUTBOX.DAT

---------- INBOX.DAT

---------- DFPDATA.DAT
[15]Silicon MegaSystems.  Enclosed is the information relating to their
[65]Silicon MegaSystems, Empire Industries, and Cain & Associates have all

---------- BUDGET83.DAT
[29]Silicon MegaSystems have ever had.  This message is being sent to you

---------- LEGAL283.DAT
[15]against Silicon MegaSystems is still pending.  The status of all

---------- REPORT.DAT
[19] Silicon MegaSystems.  However, if we look at quarterly figures by
[76]the first quarter for Silicon MegaSystems (with the greatest expenses
```

Figure 8–9. The output generated by SEARCH.BAT when "Silicon MegaSystems" is the string to be searched.

Example: An AUTOEXEC.BAT file

AUTOEXEC.BAT files are a very convenient way to execute a number of commands every time a system startup is performed. For example, many memory expansion boards contain clock-calendars. The boards come with diskettes containing programs used with the clock-calendars. One of these programs instructs DOS to get the current date and time from the clock-calendar. When the program is placed in an AUTOEXEC.BAT file, this eliminates the need for manual entry of the date and time, and the system always has the correct time.

Another useful command for AUTOEXEC.BAT files is PATH. This command tells DOS to search in specified directories for any command, program, or batch filename that is entered and not found in the current directory. For example, suppose a user frequently issues external DOS commands such as EDLIN and BACKUP, and the files that perform these operations are stored in a subdirectory called UTILITY. When this subdirectory is specified in the PATH command, EDLIN and BACKUP (and any other command or batch file in UTILITY) can be executed from any point in the directory system. The advantage of using PATH in an AUTOEXEC.BAT file is that all the search paths for frequently-used commands and batch files can be specified at once.

It also should be remembered that batch files may activate other batch routines. In an AUTOEXEC.BAT file, the last command might call up another batch routine that displays a menu, or turns on a password system. Here is an AUTOEXEC.BAT that executes a clock-calendar program, contains the PATH command, and displays a menu batch file:

```
echo off

astclock.com

path \;\utility;\sheet

cls

menu.bat
```

The commands in the above batch file have the following meaning:

echo off	This turns off the display of batch file commands.
astclock.com	This is the command for the AST Six-Pack multifunction board that tells DOS to get the current date and time from the clock-calendar on the board.
path \;\utility;\sheet	A search path is specified with this command for any command or batch file not found in the current directory. The root directory is searched first, followed by the UTILITY and SHEET subdirectories.
cls	This clears the screen, preparing it for the display of a user-designed menu.
menu.bat	This is a batch file that activates a user-designed menu.

Example: A Backup routine

Backing up fixed disk files can be greatly simplified when the commands are placed in a batch file. This is especially important when inexperienced users are required to perform regular backups. In this example, the user is required only to enter the name of the batch file and have the appropriate number of floppy diskettes ready.

```
echo off

cls

echo This routine performs a complete system backup.
```

```
echo You must have formatted diskettes ready.

echo To abort, press [Ctrl] [Break]; otherwise . . .

pause

path c:\utility

backup c: a:\/s

if errorlevel 0 echo Backup successful...
```

The first two lines of this batch file turn off the display of the batch file commands and clear the screen. The next four lines display messages. The PATH command is useful because it sets the search path for commands not found in the current directory. In this case, BACKUP is stored in the UTIL-ITY subdirectory. The next-to-last line of the above batch file performs the backup. The last line causes the message "Backup successful" to be displayed if the backup has been completed successfully.

A similar batch file could be constructed that performs backups on selected directories. The reader should consult Chapter 9 for more information on the BACKUP command.

8.6. More Rules: Batch File Commands, Replaceable Parameters, AUTOEXEC.BAT

1. Replaceable command parameters are represented in batch files using the percent symbol (%) followed by a single number from 0 to 9.
2. The %0 replaceable parameter is reserved for designating the name of the batch file itself. It may not be used for any other purpose. The numbering for all other replaceable parameters begins with %1, incrementing sequentially for each additional replaceable parameter (%2, %3,..., %9).
3. If the replaceable parameter represents a directory path, be sure to include the appropriate backslash characters (\). They may be placed in the batch file itself or they may be included with the pathname on the command line that executes the batch routine.
4. Spaces or commas separate the "real" parameters and the batch file-name when a batch file with replaceable parameters is executed.
5. The period (.) may be used as a substitute for the REM command in DOS 2.X.
6. The ECHO OFF command inhibits only the display of batch file commands. It has no effect on the display of information generated by particular batch file commands.

7. DOS automatically returns to the ECHO ON mode when a batch file is ended if ECHO OFF has been in effect.

8. The execution of the batch file may halted during the PAUSE command by pressing the [Ctrl] [Break] keys.

9. The CLS command is not restricted to batch files. It may be used anywhere in DOS.

10. Path names are not allowed in the filespec parameter of the IF command. The filespec consists of a filename and an optional filename extension.

11. Be sure to use the double equal signs (= =) in the IF command's string1 = =string2 condition.

12. The IF command's string1 = =string2 condition requires equivalence in upper- and lower-case letters for the condition to be considered true.

13. The IF command's ERRORLEVEL condition tests for the existence of error codes at the specified level or higher.

14. The labels used in the GOTO batch file command should be from one to eight characters in length. They may be longer than eight characters, but DOS recognizes only the first eight characters.

15. Batch file labels must begin with a colon (:), although the colon is not included with the label in the GOTO command. Labels are never displayed when batch files are executed.

16. The variable parameter in the FOR command must consist of two percent signs followed by a single upper- or lower-case letter (e.g., %%a).

17. Directory paths are not allowed in the set parameter of the FOR command in DOS 2.X; they are permitted in DOS 3.X. Each item in this list of files must be separated by a space, and the entire list is enclosed in parentheses. Global filename characters may be used.

18. The PROMPT command can be used to control the system prompt.

19. The AUTOEXEC.BAT file must be contained in the root directory.

9.

Creating a Menu System

With a little imagination, one can design his or her own multifunction fixed disk workstation. Various software packages and file management utilities can be easily accessed and integrated through a menu system. Previous chapters have placed emphasis on utilization of both the XT's and the AT's full potential. A user-created menu system is the vehicle by which this information can be made accessible to users of all levels.

A menu system is one of the most useful tools a new user can encounter. If designed with the user in mind, a menu can serve as a guide to all of the normal operations required for managing a fixed disk system. A well-designed menu provides the user with a discrete number of choices; these choices are worded clearly and presented in an accessible format. It also includes a number of preprogrammed command sequences that greatly reduce the number of keystrokes and the degree of knowledge required by the typical user.

The user can buy commercially available "front-ends" or menu systems. Or menu systems can be programmed in languages such as BASIC. However, if the user is not a programmer, but is nonetheless adventurous, DOS commands can be used to create the same effect.

Although DOS is not a menu-based system, user-specific menus can be created using various features of the operating system. Recent versions of DOS allow the user to take advantage of the capabilities of a tree-structured directory system. This structure provides an ideal basis for the design of a hierarchically organized menu system. By utilizing the full capabilities of batch files and exploring DOS's extended keyboard control features, one can design a surprisingly sophisticated menu system. Such a menu system can provide a much-needed interface between the user and the operating system.

9.1. Advantages of a Menu System

A well-designed menu system is a useful tool for the novice user for four main reasons: 1) a menu system greatly simplifies the use of the fixed disk,

2) it increases the efficiency of the user, 3) it can be used to organize files and directories into logical components, and 4) it provides a certain amount of control over file management and fixed disk operation. Each of these advantages is discussed briefly below.

Ease of Use

A menu system greatly reduces the amount of technical knowledge that the user must have to use the operating system effectively and to manage the fixed disk. By building many of DOS's features and commands into a menu system, the user can perform a variety of functions without having to use a reference manual. Many of DOS's more advanced features (redirection of input and output, keyboard control, etc.) can be packaged in a manner that makes them far more accessible to the average user. Furthermore, if considerable attention is given to the language used to describe menu commands and prompts, a well-designed menu system can reduce trial-and-error file management to a minimum.

––––––––––––––––––––––––––– *Example 9–1.* –––––––––––––––––––––––––––

A menu system can provide the user with the following file management/utility function options:

```
**********File Management Menu**********


        A.   Copy files

        B.   Delete files

        C.   Combine files

        D.   Sort files

        E.   Backup files
```

Each one of these options can produce a submenu; the submenu can provide the user with multiple options under that heading and further descriptions of these choices. Consider choice C, "Combine files." A submenu can give the user two choices for combining ASCII files: 1) add all files to the primary file in the order listed, or 2) combine all files in the order listed into a *new* file. The fact that these tasks utilize a variation of the COPY command, replaceable parameters, and an ASCII switch setting would be transparent to the user.

Efficiency

An easy-to-understand "front-end" to DOS not only eliminates a great deal of guesswork, but it also can significantly increase the efficiency of the system's operation. DOS batch files allow many commands to be combined into a single operation. Lengthy file management processes can be streamlined into a few steps, particularly when replaceable parameters and global filename characters are used with batch files.

─────────────────────────**Example 9–2.**─────────────────────────

Suppose a menu system contains the option "Archive Files." This option then produces three choices:

A. `Archive all files on the fixed disk`

B. `Archive all files in a directory`

C. `Archive individual files`

Using the batch file called "ARCHIVE.BAT:"

`backup c:\%1\*.* a:`

menu choice B would display the following screen and prompt the user for the name of a directory:

```
***************************************************************

              ARCHIVE DIRECTORY FILES

***************************************************************

This is a routine to archive all files within a single

directory. At the prompt, type the command "ARCHIVE," and

the name of the directory to be archived. Separate the

command and the directory name with a comma.


ENTER ARCHIVE COMMAND:
```

To back up all files in the "database" directory, for example, the user would type:

`archive,database`

Organization of Files and Directories

The hierarchical directory features of DOS allow the user to divide the fixed disk into manageable and logical components. Maintaining this organization when there are multiple users and multiple applications can be an unwieldy process. A menu system that draws upon DOS's directory organization commands gives the user two main advantages: 1) a menu "front-end" directs the user to the appropriate directory or subdirectory, thus eliminating a lot of misdirected searching activity, and 2) it provides an upfront organizational framework, thereby giving multiple users an ongoing structure in which to fit new applications and/or files. In effect, a menu system documents the organization of the fixed disk for the user.

Control

A significant advantage of a menu system is the degree of control it places over file management procedures. A menu can go a long way towards standardizing procedural sequences, particularly when there are inexperienced and/or multiple users. Also, by building command sequences into batch files that are activated by menu choices, a menu ensures that procedures are performed correctly. For example, the proper use of the BACKUP and RESTORE commands could be critical to the integrity of a fixed disk system. The controls imposed by a well-designed menu system also decrease the likelihood of inadvertent disasters. By presenting menu options that clearly describe and activate commands such as ERASE, DEL, and FORMAT, a number of potential disasters can be avoided.

9.2. What to Include in a Menu System

A well-designed menu system is tailored to the users' specific needs. This makes it difficult to determine exactly what should be contained in a generic menu system. Hence, this section will only suggest some elements that one might want to incorporate into the design of a menu system.

Main Menu

A well-designed menu system should begin with a Main Menu. This is the master menu that controls access to a number of different submenus. Inclusion of a Main Menu is desirable because it allows the designer to limit the initial menu screen to a few primary choices instead of having to fill the screen with seemingly unrelated options. The Main Menu is also important because it is the user's first introduction to the general organization of the fixed disk.

──────────────────────────── *Example 9–3.* ────────────────────────

A Main Menu screen might appear as follows:

```
***********MAIN MENU***********


1.   Software Menu

2.   File Management Menu

3.   Backup Menu

4.   HELP Menu

5.   Operating System (DOS)
```

Such a Main Menu indicates to the user that the fixcd disk is organized by software applications and contains file management utilities that are "preprogrammed" into the system. The inclusion of the HELP menu is a further clue that the user is working on a fixed disk system with an organizational plan.

Software Selections

One of the most obvious elements to include in a menu system is a software selection submenu. This submenu presents the user with the software available on the fixed disk. Each software application can be contained in a separate directory and further divided into subdirectories if necessary.

──────────────────────────── *Example 9–4.* ────────────────────────

A Software Menu might contain the following applications:

```
*************SOFTWARE MENU**************


A.   Spreadsheet/Graphics: Lotus 1-2-3

B.   Word Processing: MultiMate

C.   Database: PC-File III
```

Each of these choices could automatically place the user in a separate directory or subdirectory containing the application programs and the application data files. For example, the Software Menu might reside in a directory called "C:\software." The menu choices might then appear in the following subdirectories:

```
Lotus 1-2-3    C:\software\sheet
MultiMate      C:\software\typing
PC File III    C:\software\database
```

DOS Command Batch Files Used for File Management Utilities

A menu system also might contain a number of file management options. By using batch files, primary file management command sequences could be provided for the user. Such "preprogrammed" command sequences eliminate the need to be conversant with DOS's commands and advanced features.

───────────────────── *Example 9–5.* ─────────────────────

Many utility functions could be provided for the user, and at first it might indeed be difficult to anticipate what commands would be the most useful. A File Management Menu might contain the following choices:

```
**********FILE MANAGEMENT MENU**********


A.   Copy files

B.   Erase files

C.   Rename files

D.   Sort file listings

E.   Combine files

F.   Display directories/files
```

Each one of these choices could produce a number of options. Some of these utilities require the use of External DOS commands. All External commands might be resident in a directory called \DOS. To activate a utility requiring an External DOS command with DOS 2.X, PATH C:\DOS could be incorporated into the batch file. If constructed using DOS 3.X, the directory and pathname (\DOS) could be specified preceding the external command.

Backup and Upload Options

The fixed disk can fail at any time. Regardless of how the fixed disk is organized, backup capabilities are an absolutely essential component of any fixed disk system. A number of mechanisms (both hardware- and software-related) are available for backing up the fixed disk. The BACKUP command in DOS is but one of these alternatives. Another solution that is gaining in popularity is to use a mainframe system as a file server and upload files to the mainframe for safekeeping. Whatever backup mechanism is used, a menu choice that automatically executes a backup routine is an invaluable asset. As described above in the control-related advantages to a menu system, menu options for system backup can help ensure that the backup function is performed correctly.

On-line HELP Facilities

One can get very creative in the design of help facilities for a fixed disk system. The extent to which the system and its various applications can be documented on-line is limited only by disk space considerations. Some form of system description or help facility should be made available—particularly if the system is to be used by multiple users. The DOS text editor (EDLIN) or any other text editor can be used to create text files documenting all aspects of the system, thereby eliminating the need for printed documentation.

────────────────── *Example 9–6.* ──────────────────

A HELP Menu can be one option on a Main Menu screen. This HELP Menu might contain the following options:

```
***********HELP MENU***********


A.   Disk Organization Help

B.   Filenaming Conventions

C.   DOS Reference Guide
```

Choice A could contain a complete description of the menu system batch files and the hierarchical organization of the directories and subdirectories. A description of the hierarchical structure, for example, could be created by using EDLIN. Choice B might contain the documentation that outlines the filenaming conventions in effect for this particular fixed disk system. Choice

C might contain a summary of DOS commands and a page number reference for each command in the DOS manual(s).

Loops Back to the Main Menu or Previous Menu

A well-designed menu system will allow the user to return to the higher level menu or the Main Menu without rebooting the system. It is recommended that each menu contain an option that performs this function. In order to provide consistency from screen to screen, it may be necessary to always include a loop-back as the first option. Thus, even though menu screens may vary in size from two to six options, a loop-back option is always choice A. For example, the loop-back option on the Main Menu might read "Exit to DOS." In contrast, a loop-back option for a submenu might read "Return to Main Menu."

Other Menu Features

Menus also could be added for the use of various external devices. Options might include redirection of the output from the display to the printer, activation of the GRAPHICS command, and so on.

The number of features one can design into a menu system is limited only by the designer's creativity. Indeed, if one really wanted to get creative, a "System Messages" menu option could be designed that would allow the last user of the system to leave messages for subsequent users. This option might include three choices: 1) "Do you want to view messages?"; 2) "Do you want to remove old messages?"; or 3) "Do you want to add to existing messages?". DOS batch files could be designed to support each of those options. The menu designer is encouraged to experiment with all kinds of possibilities!

9.3. Menu Design Using Batch Files

Batch files are the key to creating an easy-to-maintain menu system. They can be activated by typing only the filename (and not the extension). For example, the batch file "ARCHIVE.BAT" is activated by simply typing the word "archive" after the system prompt. Batch files also allow the user to chain together a number of DOS commands that can be executed with a single command. These two features of batch files allow the user to create a fairly sophisticated menu system—all within the operating system.

Chaining Together Batch Files

Creating a menu system using batch files begins with the AUTOEXEC.-BAT file. This file can be used for two purposes: 1) to display Main Menu choices, and 2) to customize the system prompt. Menu screens that display the user's choices can be created using EDLIN (see Figure 9–1).

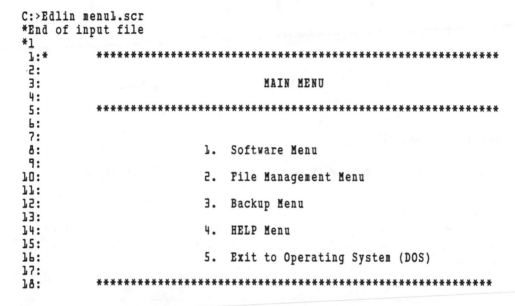

Figure 9–1. A simple Main Menu screen as it appears in EDLIN, the DOS text editor.

A four-line AUTOEXEC.BAT file can be written that displays the Main Menu screen and prompts the user for a selection:

```
echo off

cls

type menu.scr

prompt ENTER SELECTION PLEASE $g
```

This AUTOEXEC.BAT file turns off the command line display, clears the screen, types the MENU.SCR file created with EDLIN, and changes the prompt from C> to "ENTER SELECTION PLEASE>". The resulting screen display is presented in Figure 9–2.

```
************************************************************

                        MAIN MENU

************************************************************


              1.   Software Menu

              2.   File Management Menu

              3.   Backup Menu

              4.   HELP Menu

              5.   Exit to Operating System (DOS)

************************************************************

ENTER SELECTION PLEASE >
```

Figure 9–2. The Main Menu screen in Figure 9–1 as it appears on the screen.

Note that the Main Menu screen contains choices 1 through 5. Batch files can now be written for each choice, using the choice number as the name of the batch file.

Example 9–7.

Using the Main Menu screen described above, a batch file can be created for each menu selection (e.g., 1.bat, 2.bat, and so on):

1.bat	*2.bat*
echo off	echo off
cls	cls
cd\software	cd\utility
type software.scr	type utility.scr
prompt ENTER CHOICE $g	prompt ENTER CHOICE $g

When the user responds to the Main Menu prompt "ENTER SELECTION PLEASE," typing the selection number activates a batch file by that name. For example, by typing "1" (choosing the Software Menu), the directory is changed to "software" and a Software Menu screen (software.scr) is displayed. The user sees the prompt "ENTER CHOICE" (see Figure 9–3).

```
***********************************************************
                    SOFTWARE MENU
***********************************************************

        A.   Spreadsheet/Graphics:  Lotus 1-2-3

        B.   Word Processing:  MultiMate

        C.   Database:  PC-File III

        D.   Return to Main Menu

***********************************************************
```

ENTER CHOICE >

Figure 9–3. A simple Software submenu that is produced by a choice from the Main Menu.

The hierarchical nature of the menu system is apparent in the Software submenu screen. The user now has a choice of three different types of software. By typing the selection letter, another batch file is activated.

——————————————*Example 9–8.*——————————————

Suppose that the user chose selection A in the menu presented in Figure 9–3. This would activate the A.bat file with the following commands:

```
echo off

cls

cd\software\lotus

prompt $n$g

lotus

cd\

type menu.scr

prompt ENTER SELECTION:
```

This batch file performs the following functions:

1) It changes the current directory to the subdirectory where the Lotus 1-2-3 programs reside (C:\software\lotus).
2) It changes the system prompt from "ENTER CHOICE" back to "C>" so that the C> prompt is displayed if the user exits the lotus programs.

3) It activates the Lotus 1-2-3 file called "LOTUS.COM," which in turn brings the user into the Lotus Access System (1-2-3's Main Menu System).

4) It changes the directory back to the root directory when the user exits Lotus. Then it displays the Main Menu with a prompt.

Architecture of a Batch File Menu System

In each of the Main Menu batch files described above (i.e., 1.bat and 2.bat), one line of the batch file changes the directory by using the CD\ command. Both the submenu screen (e.g., software.scr) and the batch files corresponding to the menu selections are located in the directory called "software." By using separate directories for each submenu, there can be a number of files with the same name (e.g., an "A.bat" in each of five directories). Otherwise, in order to activate a unique batch file, each selection in each submenu would require a different number or letter. The architecture of a sample menu system is presented in Figure 9–4.

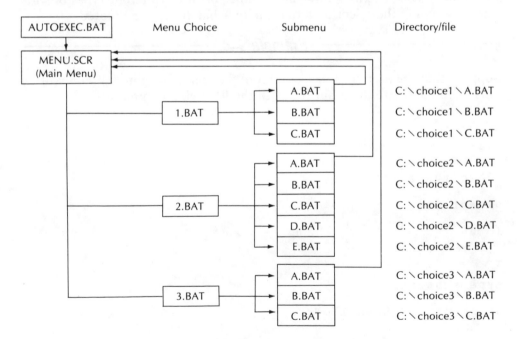

Figure 9–4. Architecture of a batch file menu system.

The example shown in Figure 9–4 includes a Main Menu with three choices and three submenus with eleven choices. Different directories for each Main Menu selection allow multiple files with the same name (e.g., there are three "A.BAT" files). As evident in Figure 9–4, a hierarchical menu system with many levels could be created using batch files and DOS's tree-structured directory features.

The example shown in Figure 9–4 also shows a loop-back feature that allows the user to return to the Main Menu from each submenu. This is the "A.BAT" choice on each submenu. An example of such a batch file is described in Example 9–9.

───────────────**Example 9–9.**───────────────

A batch file that returns the user to the Main Menu from the submenu has to perform two tasks: 1) it must change the submenu directory back to the root directory (C:\); 2) it must redisplay the Main Menu screen.

A.bat

```
echo off

cls

cd\

type menu.scr
```

The "cd\" command returns the user to the default or root directory. The "type menu.scr" command redisplays the Main Menu.

The loop-back batch file in Figure 9–4 is always selection "A" so that the option is consistently named in all submenus.

A Summary of Procedures Used to Create a Menu System

1. Using the DOS text editor (EDLIN) or any other line editor, create a Main Menu screen. Number each of the selections.
2. Using the DOS Make Directory (MD) command, create a directory for each of the selections on the Main Menu.
3. In the root directory (C:\), create an AUTOEXEC.BAT file that displays the Main Menu screen and changes the system prompt to conform to the menu format.
4. Still in the root directory, create a batch file for each selection number. Name the batch files to correspond to the selection numbers (e.g., 1.bat, 2.bat, and so on). These batch files should use the Change Directory (CD) command to change the directory for each Main Menu selection.

5. In the appropriate directory (e.g., C:\software), use EDLIN to create a submenu screen. Name each selection with a letter from A to Z. The batch files described in step 4 must also contain a command that displays this submenu screen.

6. Still in the appropriate directory, create a batch file for each selection letter. Name the batch files to correspond to the selection letters (e.g., A.bat, B.bat, and so on). Note: This procedure must be performed for each of the directories created for Main Menu selections.

9.4. Menu Bells and Whistles

Thus far, menu systems have been discussed from a functional perspective (i.e., one of what they can do for the user). A number of other features can be added to a menu system to increase its effectiveness and ease of use. These are the menu bells and whistles—the ability to accentuate various elements of the screen display, to design color-coded menus, and to use DOS's graphic capabilities to produce sophisticated menu screens.

Controlling Attributes of the Display Screen

Recent versions of DOS allow the user to control various aspects of the video display through inclusion of the file ANSI.SYS. ANSI.SYS is a loadable device driver, a hardware-specific program to which DOS transfers control whenever it must access the display. It contains the American National Standards Institute set of terminal codes.

In order for DOS to recognize ANSI.SYS, it must be placed in a user-created configuration file that is resident in the root directory (an exception to this is discussed below). This configuration file, which must be called CONFIG.SYS, is read by DOS and remains in memory along with COMMAND.COM. Whenever DOS must access the video display, for example, it passes control to ANSI.SYS.

The CONFIG.SYS file is created using EDLIN. The statement "device=ansi.sys" is typed on the first line of the CONFIG.SYS file:

```
C> edlin CONFIG.SYS

New file

*1i

        1:*device=ansi.sys

        2:*^C (note: produced by entering <Ctrl-C>)

*e
```

ANSI.SYS could also be placed in a directory of DOS commands (e.g., \DOS) rather than the root directory. The first line of CONFIG.SYS would then read:

```
1:*device=\DOS\ansi.sys
```

ANSI.SYS can be used to alter various attributes of the display because it allows the user to specify control codes that determine how characters appear on the display. For example, the user can specify background and foreground colors, reverse video displays, and so on. In order to alter various attributes of the display, ANSI.SYS intercepts those control codes that begin with an escape character (ASCII 27). The escape character signals that all characters following it should be interpreted as commands. Another character also must follow the escape character in order to define the ANSI.SYS set of escape sequences that are specific to the PC. This character is the left bracket ([ ).

Thus, to incorporate various screen attributes into the design of a menu, the user must 1) be familiar with DOS's extended screen and keyboard control codes, and 2) figure out how to get an escape character into the file that controls the attribute(s).

Creating an Escape Character

The escape character is the key to performing all kinds of tricks with the video screen. It can be created in a file using EDLIN, or escape sequences can be activated by the PROMPT command. Each of these methods will be described below.

Creating an Escape Character Using EDLIN

An escape character is created by first issuing the EDLIN command. At the EDLIN prompt for line #1, simultaneously press the [Ctrl] and [V] keys. This will appear as:

```
C> edlin ESCAPE

New file

*i

1:*^V
```

(Note: "ESCAPE" is the filename)
Then press the left bracket key ([ ). The line will now appear as:

```
1:*^V[
```

The escape character is now in the file. When this file is displayed using the TYPE command, the escape character appears as:

^[

Once the escape character file (ESCAPE) is created, any codes can be added to the escape character. Each attribute file containing an escape character can be named to match its function.

────────────── *Example 9–10.* ──────────────

In order to create a file that increases the intensity of display characters, the user goes into EDLIN and creates a new file called BRIGHT.SCR. An escape character is created as described above and a control character is added. To make the display characters brighter in intensity, the code **[1m** is added to the escape character (^[):

```
C> edlin BRIGHT.SCR

New file

*i

    1:*^V[[1m

        2:*^C     (Note: produced by entering <Ctrl-C>)

*e
```

Now the user has a file named "BRIGHT.SCR" with the contents, ^[[1m. This file can be activated at any time by issuing the command:

```
type BRIGHT.SCR
```

The intensity of the next character typed will be visibly greater. All characters will remain at that intensity until a command is issued to restore the video display to its normal or default state.

Creating an Escape Character Using the PROMPT Command

Using the PROMPT command, an escape character can be placed in a batch file or used directly at the system prompt (C:\). The PROMPT command causes a string of characters to be sent to the display. Typically, its purpose is to change the prompt command on the screen. For example, if the user types

```
prompt ENTER COMMAND $g
```

the C> prompt disappears and ENTER COMMAND> appears.

A lesser understood function of the PROMPT command is its ability to activate *metastrings*. Metastrings are groups of characters that are assigned a specific meaning in DOS. They always follow the word PROMPT and begin with a dollar sign ($).

Example 9–11.

The user can change the prompt using the metastrings:

$d Displays current date
$t Displays current time
$g Produces the > prompt

Thus, the command: prompt $d tg produces the following prompt on the screen:

```
Sat 7-14-1984  18:16:04.92>
```

The one metastring of particular relevance here is the escape character ($e). This escape character is recognized by ANSI.SYS. As described above, ANSI.SYS interprets characters that follow the escape sequence as commands. Therefore, those strings that begin with the sequence $e are intercepted by ANSI.SYS and can be used to control many aspects of the display screen. The left bracket symbol ([ ) also must follow the $e metastring. Consider the following example:

Example 9–12.

The control code for reverse video (black on white) is 7m ("m" indicates that it is a character attribute). Issuing the PROMPT command with the escape character

```
prompt $e[7m
```

would cause the display to shift to a black foreground and white background. The display could be restored to normal (white on black) with the command

```
prompt $e[0m
```

where the number "0" resets the display to its normal or default attributes.

The escape character metastring also can be used in a batch file. This can be particularly useful when painting a color screen for a menu display.

_____ **Example 9–13.** _____

The following batch file paints a Main Menu screen with a blue background and a white foreground:

```
prompt $e[44m

echo off

cls

type mainmenu.scr

prompt ENTER SELECTION PLEASE $g
```

EDLIN versus PROMPT Method

Whichever method is employed to create an escape character depends on the user's needs. The authors' preferred choice is the EDLIN method for two reasons:

1. The PROMPT command, when used to send escape sequences to ANSI.SYS, does not work well with the ECHO OFF Batch file command. ECHO OFF inhibits the screen display of DOS commands. When placed in a batch file preceding a PROMPT $e commmand, ECHO OFF blocks execution of the escape sequence until the batch routine ends. This peculiarity prevents the user from producing a color menu screen using the PROMPT command while inhibiting the display of DOS commands. The net effect is an ugly menu, to say the least.

2. The escape character created in EDLIN can easily be transferred to attribute-specific files. Attribute-specific files can be identified through their filenames. For example:

RED.SCR	Produces a red screen
BLUE.SCR	Produces a blue screen
REVERSE.SCR	Produces a reverse video screen

   These attribute files then can be activated at the system level by issuing the command: type BLUE.SCR. Or, they can be activated in other batch files by including the line: type COLOR.SCR. (These procedures are described in more detail below.)

In contrast, when using the PROMPT command at the system level, the user must always remember the appropriate control codes. For example, to restore the video display to normal, the user would have to type:

```
prompt $e[[0m
```

Using Attributes to Enhance Menu Screens (Monochrome)

Various attributes can be used to visually enhance either a color or a monochrome menu. The following list of attributes and escape sequences can be used with both monochrome and color displays (the exception is LINE.SCR, which is a monochrome-only attribute):

Filename	Escape Sequence	Function
NORMAL.SCR	^[[0m	Restores display to normal attributes
OFF.SCR	^[[8m	Characters typed are invisible
BLINK.SCR	^[[5m	Produces blinking cursor
BRIGHT.SCR	^[[1m	Increases the intensity of character color
VIDEO.SCR	^[[7m	Produces a reverse video screen
LINE.SCR	^[[4m	Underscores characters

The above attributes can be used to draw attention to certain lines on an otherwise busy screen or to emphasize features of the menu. The OFF.SCR attribute file, for example, makes characters invisible and is an excellent tool for masking certain keyboard input (e.g., masking a password). And, after any of these or other attributes have been used in a menu, the NOR-MAL.SCR must be activated to restore the screen display to its default or normal condition.

Using Attributes to Enhance Menu Screens (Color)

In addition to the display attributes described above, the user can create a multitude of screen color combinations. Escape code sequences can be used to change the color of the screen (the background) and the characters displayed on the screen (the foreground). These colors can be used to enhance a menu display, color-code various elements of a menu system, or to emphasize certain features of a menu screen.

Creating a Color Palette

The user can create a color palette by building 16 files (eight screen colors and eight character colors); each one must contain an escape character and the appropriate color control code. In the color palette described below, colors are designated as either character (.CAR) or screen (.SCR). The character control code values range between 30 and 37. Screen color control codes range between 40 and 47. Corresponding character and screen colors (e.g., CYAN.CAR and CYAN.SCR) are 10 values apart (36 and 46 respectively).

Character Colors		Screen Colors	
BLACK.CAR	^[[30m	BLACK.SCR	^[[40m
BLUE.CAR	^[[34m	BLUE.SCR	^[[44m
CYAN.CAR	^[[36m	CYAN.SCR	^[[46m
GREEN.CAR	^[[32m	GREEN.SCR	^[[42m
MAGENTA.CAR	^[[35m	MAGENTA.SCR	^[[45m
RED.CAR	^[[31m	RED.SCR	^[[41m
WHITE.CAR	^[[37m	WHITE.SCR	^[[47m
YELLOW.CAR	^[[33m	YELLOW.SCR	^[[43m

Each of these colors is activated by entering the filename after the TYPE command. For example, to change the display screen to red, the user issues the command:

```
type RED.SCR
```

When this command is issued, a red background will be displayed as new characters are typed. To color the entire screen red, the user must issue the command CLS (clear screen). In order to restore the color display screen to its normal black-and-white state, the user must type NORMAL.SCR.

Color Menus

The color files described above can be placed in batch file sequences with which the user can "paint" a menu screen.

_____ *Example 9–14.* _____

Suppose that a menu is designed with the following text and color codes for each choice:

MAIN USERS' MENU	(Color)
1. Software Menu	Magenta
2. Exit to DOS	Red
3. Archive File Program	Cyan
4. HELP Screens	Green

To produce a menu display with a blue background and color-coded sections for each menu choice, the following batch file can be written:

echo off	Turns off DOS command display
type blue.scr	Paints a blue background
type black.car	Produces black characters (used to ensure visibility on all screen colors)
type main.scr	Types "MAIN USERS'MENU"
type magenta.scr	Paints a magenta screen section
type software.scr	Types "1. Software Menu"
type red.scr	Paints a red screen section
type DOS.scr	Types "2. Exit to DOS"
type cyan.scr	Paints a cyan screen section
type archive.scr	Types "3. Archive File Program"
type green.scr	Paints a green screen section
type help.scr	Types "4. HELP Screens"
prompt ENTER SELECTION $g	Produces "ENTER SELECTION >"

In order to create colored menu sections in which the appropriate text appears, each line of text was placed in a separate four-line file. For example, the file "SOFTWARE.SCR" was created with Edlin and contains the text "1. Software Menu" (on line 1); three additional blank lines (lines 2 through 4) are included in the file as well. Visually, these blank lines create a wide band of color for this menu selection.

Menu Graphics

A number of special ASCII characters can be used to create graphic designs for a menu. These characters include solid and open bar lines, corner angles, and intersecting lines (see Figure 9–5).

Each of these characters has a corresponding three-digit ASCII code. A table of these values can be found in the Appendices of the IBM BASIC reference manual. These characters are produced at the keyboard by holding down the [Alt] key and pressing the desired ASCII code digits on the numeric keypad.

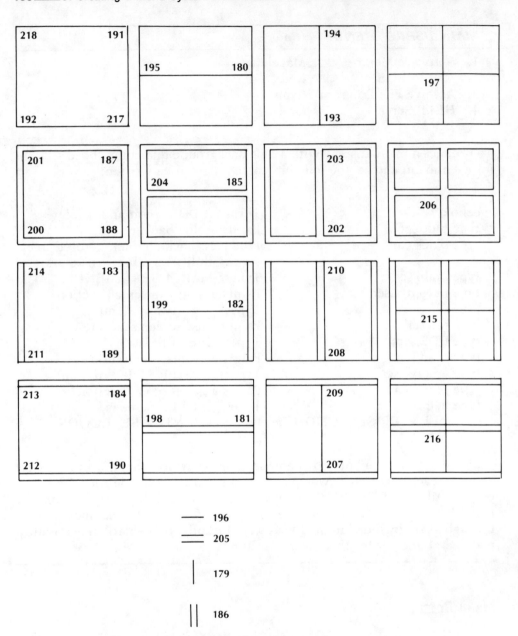

Figure 9–5. DOS's graphic capabilities may be used to create professional-looking menu screens. Various lines, borders, angles, and intersecting lines can be "drawn" using the [Alt] key and ASCII character sequences typed on the numeric keypad. These numeric codes are indicated next to each line and at each intersection of lines.

Using these characters, one can create professional-looking menus and submenus. Other ASCII characters can be experimented with to create unusual and creative designs:

[Alt] 176	[Alt] 222
[Alt] 177	[Alt] 223
[Alt] 178	[Alt] 236
[Alt] 219	[Alt] 240
[Alt] 220	[Alt] 248
[Alt] 221	[Alt] 254

The designs presented in Figures 9–6 through 9–11 were created using some of the characters listed above. There is no end to the amount of fun one can have creating checkerboard menus, cube-like designs, simulated art deco menus, and so on.

MAIN SYSTEM MENU

Figure 9–6. A menu system design.

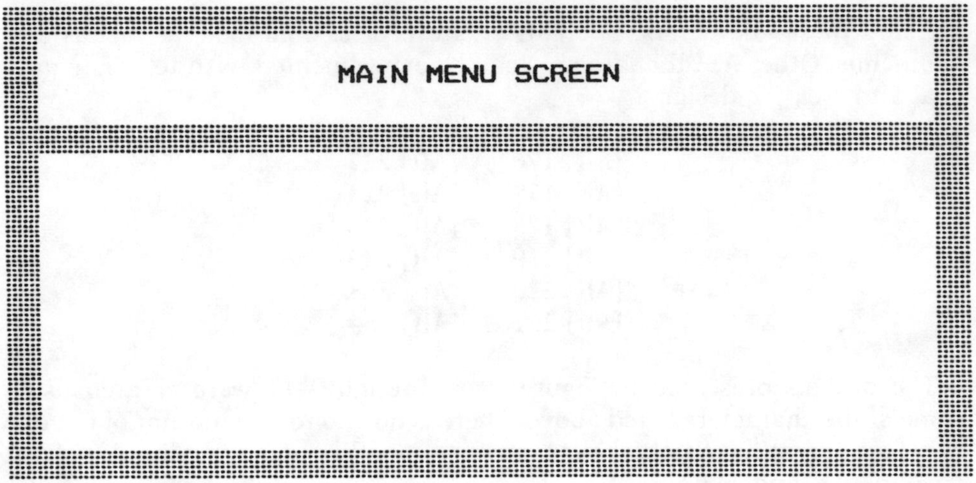

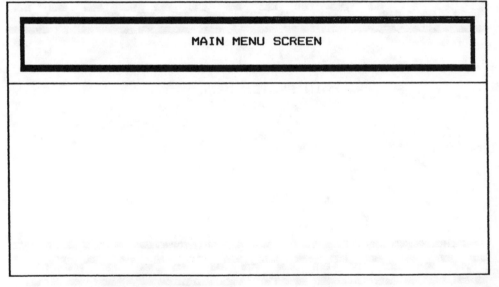

MAIN MENU SCREEN

Figure 9–7. A menu system design.

MAIN MENU SCREEN

Figure 9–8. A menu system design.

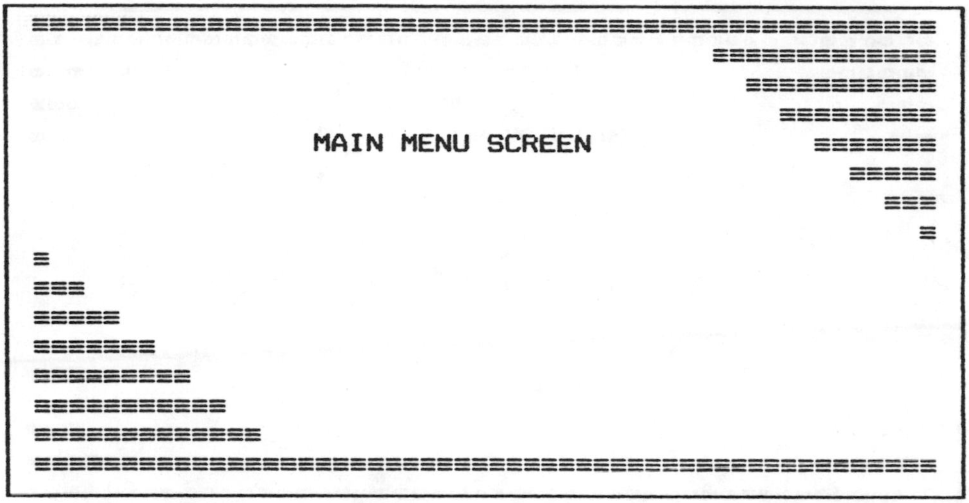

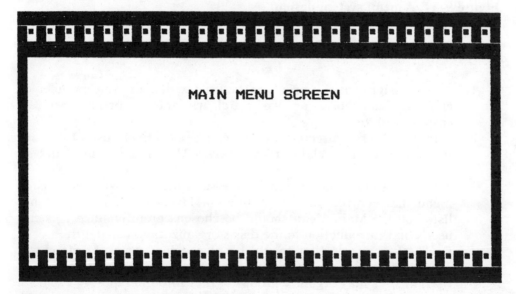

Figure 9–9. A menu system design.

MAIN MENU SCREEN

Figure 9–10. A menu system design.

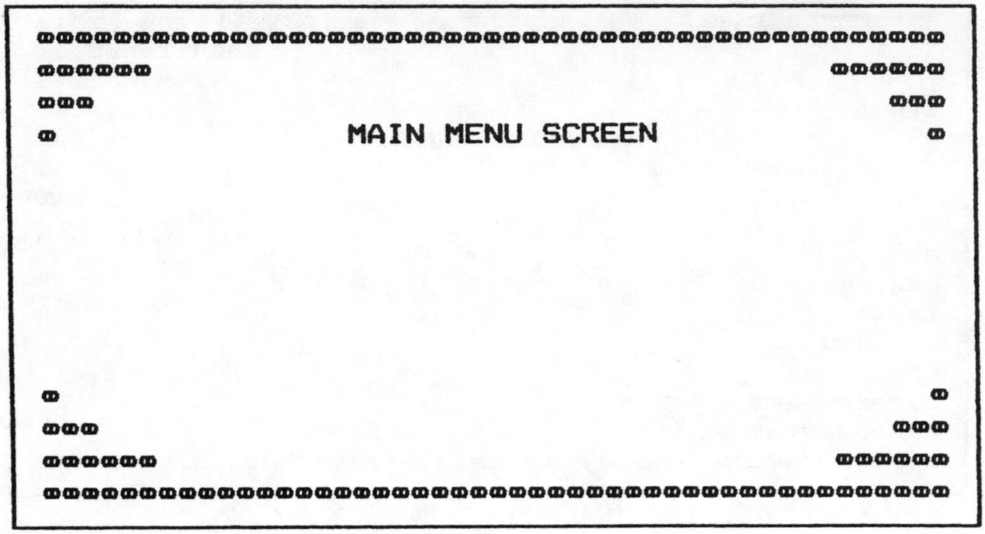

```
□□□□□□□□□□□□□□□□□□□□□□□□□□□□□□□□□□□□□□□□□□□□□□□□□□□□□□□□□□□□□□□□
□□□□□□                                                      □□□□□□
□□□                                                           □□□
□                      MAIN  MENU  SCREEN                       □



□                                                              □
□□□                                                          □□□
□□□□□                                                      □□□□□
□□□□□□□□□□□□□□□□□□□□□□□□□□□□□□□□□□□□□□□□□□□□□□□□□□□□□□□□□□□□□□□□□□
```

Figure 9–11. A menu system design.

9.5. A Summary of Tips on Creating Menus

1. A well-designed menu provides the user with a discrete number of choices; these choices are worded clearly and are presented in an easy-to-read format.
2. A tree-structured directory system can be effectively used to create many tiers of interrelated menus (Main Menus, submenus, and so on).
3. A menu system should begin with a Main Menu. This is the master menu that controls access to different layers of submenus. Items listed on the Main Menu should be chosen carefully since it is the user's first introduction to the disk's organizational structure.
4. Each software selection should be placed in a separate directory. Those directories should be further divided into subdirectories so that the user may organize groups of files into file types.
5. All menu systems should include a backup option.
6. A menu system should be designed so that the user can always return to a higher level menu or the Main Menu without rebooting the system.
7. DOS batch files are used to create a menu system. The Main Menu can be displayed when an AUTOEXEC.BAT batch file is activated. Thereafter, one batch file can call another, and so on, until all menu selections and submenus are chained together. Batch files may be created and named for each selection (e.g., 1.BAT, 2.BAT, A.BAT).

8. EDLIN or another text editor is used to create the batch files behind the menu system.

9. Various attributes of the display screen may be altered to make a menu screen more elaborate. To alter display attributes, a CONFIG.SYS file must be created; it also must contain the device driver ANSI.SYS. Control codes may be created and placed in batch files to change the color of the foreground and background, the intensity of characters, and so on.

10. Graphic designs for menus and menu borders can be created in EDLIN using ASCII characters and their corresponding ASCII character codes. A table of these three-digit codes can be found in Appendix G of the IBM BASIC reference manual. These characters are produced at the keyboard by depressing the [Alt] key and pressing the desired ASCII code digits on the *numeric* keyboard.

10.

Security Issues

Everyone who works with the XT or AT will eventually discover that information stored on the fixed disk is vulnerable. For example, data loss may result from hard disk failure, or important files may be lost or become unavailable due to system failure. On another level, a user's critical or sensitive files may be susceptible to unauthorized access unless special precautions are taken. Also, there is no built-in mechanism in either the XT or the AT that prevents files stored on the fixed disk from being duplicated illegally.

There are many ways to deal with these issues and minimize this lack of security. One may use DOS to design basic password systems schemes for hiding files. DOS also has some commands that are used for backing up files stored on the fixed disk. More sophisticated security can be achieved through the use of various hardware and software products. These products give the user the ability to limit file and system access, to create audit trails, and to prevent illegal file duplication. Other products provide highly sophisticated methods for data backup.

Data backup and security can be some of the most important aspects of XT and AT management. This chapter describes some of the options available to the user.

10.1. The AT's Built-in Security

A standard feature on the PC-AT is a security device called the *Keylock*. This is a tubular locking mechanism that is located on the front of the system unit. When locked, it prevents an unauthorized operator from using the system. The computer may be turned on, but it will not accept any keyboard input. It also prevents the system unit cover from being removed. If the computer is already running, the system can be locked and left unattended. The computer cannot be rebooted, nor will any other keystrokes be accepted. The key is difficult to duplicate.

One of the advantages of such a device is that a user can leave the computer unattended while it is performing long calculations. There is no need to worry about someone interrupting an operation or looking through the contents of sensitive files.

It should be noted that a security mechanism can be purchased and installed on the XT and the PC that locks and unlocks the system start switch. However, it does not lock the keyboard.

10.2. Using DOS to Restrict Access

Although the AT has its own built-in security, this feature is not sold with the XT. Furthermore, when an AT must be shared among many different users, it may not be practical to entrust the key for the Keylock to a single individual; it may have to be left unlocked for long periods of time. If this is the case, or if an XT is used, then it might be appropriate to add some access restrictions.

A certain amount of security can be built into an XT or an AT through the use of DOS. A basic password system can be constructed using batch files. Batch routines also may be used to disguise and hide sensitive data files.

It should be stated at the outset that these systems are not intended to prevent knowledgeable users from gaining access to a system. For these individuals, these systems are more akin to car alarms. In effect, they represent a time-consuming obstacle that may make unauthorized access more trouble than it is worth. However, these systems may provide a fair amount of security when the typical user is not particularly knowledgeable about DOS or DOS batch routines.

Designing a Password System Using DOS

Batch files can be used to design an inelegant but reasonably effective XT or AT password system. A password batch file can restrict access to a menu system. By doing so, it prevents the unauthorized user from tapping into the system's underlying directory, subdirectory, and file structures. This batch file also can activate attribute-specific escape sequences (see Chapter 9) that inhibit output to the display. Thus, it can be used to mask any information (e.g., the password) typed by the user.

Although this type of system is by no means foolproof, it has been demonstrated to be effective in several different operating environments. In lieu of a custom-programmed or commercially available password security system, it is a decent "car alarm." This section describes how to create a batch file-based password system and discusses the limitations and weaknesses of such a system.

Preparation for a Password Batch File

The first task in creating a password system is designing a password screen. This is the first screen that will be seen by the user. It should indicate that the system is password protected and should prompt the user for a password. A sample password screen is shown in Figure 10–1.

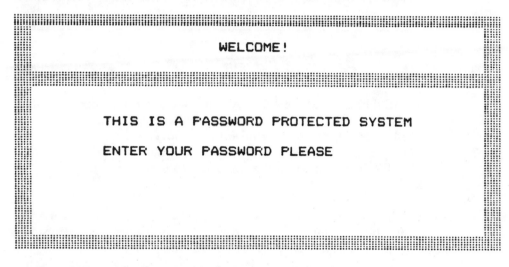

```
                        WELCOME!



         THIS IS A PASSWORD PROTECTED SYSTEM

         ENTER YOUR PASSWORD PLEASE
```

Figure 10–1. A sample password screen.

Next, attribute-specific escape sequence files must be created to turn off the display and to turn the display back on. By turning off the display, the password typed by the user is invisible on the screen. After the correct password is entered, the display must be restored to normal. These escape sequences are as follows:

^[[8m   Turns the display off
^[[0m   Restores the display to normal

Creation of these escape sequence files is discussed in Section 9.4 of the previous chapter. To reiterate, an escape character must first be created and placed in an attribute-specific file using EDLIN (the DOS text editor). This file then may be activated by the command:

`TYPE [filename.ext]`

―――――――――――――――― *Example 10–1.* ――――――――――――――――

A password system requires the creation of two attribute-specific files that contain the following escape sequences (as they appear in EDLIN):

```
Display.on                      Display.off

*1                              *1

    1:^[[0m                         1:^[[8m

    1:*                             1:*
```

These two files can now be activated from within the password system batch files.

Architecture of a Password System

The user's initial entry into the XT or AT can be controlled through use of an AUTOEXEC.BAT file. DOS scans the root directory (C:\) for an AUTOEXEC.BAT file after it loads itself into memory.

The first thing that DOS does is execute the commands contained in that file. This AUTOEXEC.BAT file can be modified to serve two functions in a password system:

1. Display the password screen and prompt the user for a password.
2. Turn off the display by activating an attribute-specific escape sequence (e.g., the file "Display.off" described above).

In this password system, the password is simply the name of the batch file. Whenever the user types the correct password (batch file name), the Main Menu screen appears. The architecture of such a system is shown in Figure 10–2.

The rationale behind such a design is as follows:

1. The AUTOEXEC.BAT file, which is the user's entry point into the system, prompts the user for a password through a password screen. It then turns the display screen OFF. If the user attempts to break out of the batch routine at this point, the screen display remains invisible. The user must reboot the system, which will return him or her to the password screen.
2. The password is the batch file name. Batch files can be activated by typing the filename (without an extension). This password can easily be changed, using the DOS RENAME command.

Event	Flow	Function
	AUTOEXEC.BAT	
1) System is boot-ed and the AUTOEX-EC.BAT file is activated.	echo off type password.scr type display.off	Turns off DOS cmmd display Displays password screen Turns off screen display
2) User must re-spond with cor-rect password Incorrect pass-words produce no response.	User types password (password is batch file name; e.g., "gi-raffe")	
	GIRAFFE.BAT	
3) Correct pass-word activates batch file by that name. MAIN MENU screen appears.	echo off type display.on prompt $d $t type mainmenu.scr prompt ENTER CHOICE:	Turns off DOS cmmd display Turns screen display on Prompts user for date/time Displays the MAIN MENU Prompts user for selection

Figure 10–2. Architecture of a password system

3. The display screen is not restored to normal until the correct password is entered. Only then is the user prompted for the date and time. Placing this function after the password entry point eliminates the ability of the user to circumvent the password by pressing [Ctrl] [Break] at the date or time prompt.

4. The password batch file is the user's access to the Main Menu (or to applications software if no menu exists). The Main Menu can be used to further control access to directories, subdirectories, and specific files.

Changing the Password

A short batch file can be written that allows the average user to change his or her password without being conversant in DOS. An example is described below:

——————————————————**Example 10–2.**——————————————————

In order to change a password, the user types "PASSWORD" at the C> prompt. This activates a batch file named "PASSWORD.BAT" that prompts the user for the desired change.

```
echo off

cls

echo      ********************************************************

echo                      PASSWORD CHANGE

echo      ********************************************************

echo      This is a routine to change your system password. At the

echo      prompt,type the command "CHANGE" followed by the OLD and

echo      NEW passwords. Separate the command "CHANGE," the old

echo      password, and the new password with commas.

prompt ENTER PASSWORD CHANGE COMMAND:
```

The batch file shown above produces the screen display presented in Figure 10–3.

```
************************************************************
                     PASSWORD CHANGE
************************************************************
This is a routine to change your system password. At the
prompt, type the command "CHANGE" followed by the OLD and
NEW passwords.  Separate the command "CHANGE," the old
password, and the new password with commas.
 ENTER PASSWORD CHANGE COMMAND:change,giraffe,betta
```

Figure 10–3. The password change prompt and the user's input as they appear on the display screen.

When the user responds to the prompt, e.g., by typing "CHANGE, giraffe, betta," a second batch file, CHANGE.BAT, is activated:

──────────────────── *Example 10–3.* ────────────────────

```
echo off

cls

prompt $n$g

rename %1.bat %2.bat

echo          New Password is: %2

echo          Type the command "CLS" at the prompt to exit.
```

The batch file, CHANGE.BAT, produces the display shown in Figure 10–4. CHANGE.BAT uses replaceable parameters (%1 and %2) for the old and new passwords, respectively. The new password (%2) is then displayed and the user is instructed how to exit the routine.

```
New Password is: betta
Type the command "CLS" at the prompt to exit.
```

Figure 10–4. Screen display of the new password along with instructions to exit the password change routine.

Control Weaknesses

As mentioned at the outset, such a system is merely a deterrent for the average user. Three principal control weaknesses are described below. In each case, once the intruder gets past the password, he or she must still decipher the layout, organization, and hierarchical structure of the fixed disk.

1. The intruder can insert his or her own DOS disk into Drive A and boot the system off of the A drive. The intruder would then have to issue the TREE commmand, obtain directory listings, and search from there.
2. The intruder could use the [Ctrl] [PrtSc] keys to direct the display output to the printer. This would allow him or her to print out the TREE command and directory listings to search for the password. The password or an attribute-specific escape sequence file would have to be detected in order for the intruder to restore the display screen to normal.
3. The most serious control weakness is the intruder's ability to interrupt the batch routine before the display.off command is activated. This is done by pressing [Ctrl] [Break] *immediately* as the system is booted. You have to be quick, but, unfortunately, it works.

Hiding and Disguising Files

A basic mechanism for preventing access to specific files is through batch routines that hide a file by changing its filename, filename extension, or its location in the directory system. When a fixed disk contains a number of files, even sophisticated users may find unauthorized access to these files extraordinarily difficult. Several batch routines are described below that use these techniques.

Assigning New Filenames and Filename Extensions

On the simplest level, a sensitive file can be assigned a new filename that disguises its real content. This can be done manually, or the procedure could be automated in a batch file.

A more effective way of hiding a file is to change the filename extension. Most applications programs require that their data files have certain types of filename extensions in order to be read. For example, 1-2-3 worksheet files must have .WKS as their extensions, or they will not be "seen" by the program. If a sensitive 1-2-3 file is given a different extension, the unauthorized user must find the file in DOS and change its extension back to a 1-2-3 format before it can be viewed in 1-2-3. If the encrypted extension is common to many other files on the system, this could be a very time-consuming task.

There are a number of components that should be built into batch routines that change filenames and filename extensions:

1. Replaceable parameters should be used to specify the filenames or filename extensions in the batch file. This allows many files to be encrypted with the same generic batch file.

2. A record or log of the changes should be maintained. The system manager may wish to store this information on the fixed disk in a separate file, or record it on a floppy diskette. This is particularly important if numerous files are encrypted.
3. There should be a batch routine that restores the original filename extension to an encrypted file. This makes it easier for authorized users to gain access to the files.

The sample batch routine shown below is designed to disguise data files so that they may not be accessed by different software programs. The filenames are left intact in the "encryption" process, but the filename extensions are changed.

───── Example 10–4. ─────

In order to change a filename extension, the user types "HIDE" at the C> prompt. This activates the following batch file named "HIDE.BAT," which instructs the user how to change the filename extension:

```
echo off

cls

echo      ************************************************************

echo                CHANGE FILENAME EXTENSION

echo      ************************************************************

echo      This is a routine to change a filename extension. At the

echo      prompt,type the command "ENCRYPT" followed by the name

echo      of the file whose extension is to be changed. Do NOT

echo      type the extension. Separate the command "ENCRYPT" and

echo      the filename with a comma.

prompt ENTER "ENCRYPTION" CHANGE COMMAND:
```

The batch file in the above example produces the screen display shown in Figure 10–5. Suppose the extension of a file named BUDGET.WKS is changed. The user responds to the prompt displayed in the above routine by entering the command:

```
encrypt,budget
```

This activates the following batch file in Example 10–6.

Example 10–6.

```
echo off

dir %1.*>>\utility\record.con

rename %1.* %1.con
```

The second line of this batch file records the original filename and extension in a file called RECORD.CON. This file is located in the UTILITY directory. The global filename character allows any filename extension to be changed. The RENAME command in the third line of the batch file changes the extension. The user knows that all files listed in RECORD.CON have been "encrypted" with a new file extension of .CON.

```
**************************************************************
                    CHANGE FILENAME EXTENSION
**************************************************************
This is a routine to change a filename extension. At the
prompt, type the command "ENCRYPT" followed by the name of
the file whose extension is to be changed. Do NOT type
the extension. Separate the command "ENCRYPT" and the
filename with a comma.
 ENTER "ENCRYPTION" CHANGE COMMAND:
```

Figure 10–5. Screen display generated for the change filename extension "encryption" routine.

Restoring the Filename Extension

Example 10–7 describes the batch routine that restores a filename extension back to its original form.

─────────────────── *Example 10–7.* ───────────────────

In order to restore the original extension to a filename, the user types the command "REVEAL." This activates the "REVEAL.BAT" batch file, which is shown below:

```
echo off

cls

echo        **********************************************************

echo                     RESTORE FILENAME EXTENSION

echo        **********************************************************

echo        This is a routine to restore a filename extension to its

echo        original format. At the prompt, type the command

echo        "DECRYPT" followed by the file whose extension is to be

echo        restored and the file's original extension. Separate

echo        the command "DECRYPT," the filename, and the filename

echo        extension with commas.

prompt ENTER "DECRYPTION" COMMAND:
```

Suppose the user wants to restore the original extension to the BUDGET.WKS file, which was renamed BUDGET.CON in the previous section. The user responds to the prompt displayed in the above batch file by entering the command:

```
decrypt,budget,wks
```

This would activate yet another batch file (see Example 10–8).

─────────────────── *Example 10–8.* ───────────────────

```
echo off

rename %1.con %1.%2
```

This batch file replaces the .CON filename extension with the one specified by the user. In this case, .CON is replaced by .WKS.

Changing the Location of a File

Another method for hiding files is to change the location of the file in the directory hierarchy. This can be particularly effective when the file also is given a new filename extension. The hidden file might be placed in a subdirectory where all files have the same extension. If the target file also has the same extension, its presence may not be easily detected, even by experienced users. An intruder has to try reading each file with the appropriate application program before discovering that it does not belong.

Example 10–9 shows a batch routine that renames a file with a different filename extension and moves it to a different directory.

_____**Example 10–9.**_____

This batch file renames files with the .WKS extension (1-2-3 files) with the BASIC program's extension of .BAS. The file then is copied to the directory containing the BASIC files and erased from its original location. Replaceable parameters allow the use of different filenames. The original filename is recorded in a file called RECORD.CON.

```
echo off

dir %1>>record.con

rename %1.wks %1.bas

copy %1.bas \basfiles

erase %1.bas
```

If the above batch file is called MOVE.BAT, a 1-2-3 file called BUDGET.WKS can be renamed and moved to a directory called BASFILES with the following command:

```
move,budget
```

When an attempt is made to run the renamed 1-2-3 file in BASIC, the file can be loaded, but nothing happens when the RUN command is entered. Attempting to run a foreign file in a program may not always produce predictable results. It is suggested that the user test the effect of this on a dummy file before it is incorporated into a batch routine.

Using the ATTRIB Command (DOS 3.X)

The DOS command ATTRIB (Attribute) can be used to protect sensitive files from inadvertent erasure. It is available only in DOS 3.0 or later. This command allows a file to be marked as Read-Only, which means that the file can be read, but any attempts to alter or erase it will fail. The command has the following format:

```
[d:][path]ATTRIB [+/-R] [d:][path]filename[.ext]
```

The parameters of this command have the following meaning:

d: This specifies the disk drive. Before the ATTRIB command, it designates the disk drive containing the ATTRIB command; after the ATTRIB command, it designates the drive of the file whose read/write status is to be changed. If no drive is specified, then the default drive is used.

path   Before the ATTRIB command, it designates a specific directory in the directory hierarchy where the ATTRIB command is located; after the ATTRIB, it specifies the directory location of the file whose attribute is to be changed. If no path is specified, then the current directory is used.

filename A single file may be designated. More than one file may be specified through the use of global filename characters.

.ext   This specifies the filename extension. Global filename characters may be used.

+/−R   This sets the attribute of the file(s). When +R is specified, the file is marked as Read-Only; when -R is specified, the file is marked as read/write. If this parameter is omitted, the status of the file will be displayed; the output for Read-Only files will show an "R" in front of the filename.

Suppose the system manager would like to protect an important database file against possible erasure or unauthorized change. If the file is called DATABASE.WKS, and is located in a directory called \SHEET, the command might be entered as follows:

```
attrib +r \sheet\database.wks
```

If the ATTRIB command is not located in the current directory, the drive and path could precede the command. Suppose that the command for the above example is located in the \UTIL directory. The command then would be written as:

```
c:\util\attrib +r \sheet\database.wks
```

Once the attribute has been set to Read-Only, any attempt to alter or erase the file will result in the DOS error message "Access denied." The error message may be different when erasure or alteration is attempted from within an application program.

10.3. Fixed Disk Backup Using DOS

The user has a number of protection options to guard against irreparable data loss. DOS has several commands that can be used to create backup copies of the fixed disk on floppy diskettes. This procedure is known as a "system backup." For most users, these commands can provide adequate security against loss of data through fixed disk or system failure. However, this security is effective only when these routines are performed regularly.

The nature of the data on the fixed disk determines how often a system backup ought to be performed. For example, if several individuals use and update many files on a daily basis, then a system backup should be performed at least once a week. In a situation such as this, it is not likely that regular backups will be performed unless one person has been given the responsibility for this task.

A higher level of data security can be provided through the use of special hardware devices. These devices typically use tapes or cartridges as the storage medium. The factors that differentiate this type of security from a DOS backup are a function of reliability, speed, automation, and cost.

This section describes the ways that the user may prevent data loss using DOS. The following section discusses the hardware devices that provide even greater security against data loss.

Typical Calamities

Probably first on the list of events that cause data loss is hard disk failure. *All hard disks fail eventually.* Although most fixed disks can be expected to last many years, a new fixed disk occasionally fails after only a few months of use. Poor maintenance can greatly facilitate this. For example, failure to run the Relocation program on the IBM Diagnostics diskette before moving the XT or AT system unit is one way to reduce a fixed disk's life span. This program repositions the heads in the fixed disk to prevent the heads from crashing onto the disk surfaces while in transit. The user should always run this program before moving the system unit.

Failure of the system unit may not affect data stored on the fixed disk, but it can make it temporarily unavailable. Like the fixed disk, various components in the system unit can break down occasionally. For example, problems may develop in multi-function boards or in peripherals such as the keyboard, or chips in the memory banks may become defective.

Data loss also can be the result of less predictable events: The computer may be stolen; an important file may be inadvertently overwritten by another file with the same filename; a file may be accidentally erased.

In all of these events, appropriate backup measures can prevent a minor inconvenience from escalating to a major crisis. Unfortunately, a catastrophe of some sort is often required before the habit of making regular backups is formed.

DOS Backup Procedures

There are several ways to create floppy diskette backups of files stored on the fixed disk. The COPY command is one method. Files can be copied onto a floppy diskette, either one by one or as a group, by using global filename characters. There are several limitations to this approach: First, the COPY command cannot be used when a fixed disk file is larger than the capacity of the floppy diskette; second, if the COPY command uses global filename characters, all of the files included under the global filename must fit onto a single diskette, or the process will halt when the diskette is full.

DOS provides the user with another method of creating floppy diskette backups that eliminates these problems: This approach involves the use of two special commands, BACKUP and RESTORE. With the BACKUP command, the user may copy one or more fixed disk files onto one or more floppy diskettes. RESTORE copies these backups from the floppies back onto the fixed disk. Each command is discussed below.

The BACKUP command

BACKUP copies fixed disk files to floppy diskettes in a special format that allows a single file to occupy more than one diskette. Files copied with the BACKUP command may be used only after they have been processed through the RESTORE command. Floppy diskettes must be formatted before files are copied onto them with BACKUP. The BACKUP command is written as follows:

```
BACKUP [d:][path][filename][.ext] d:[/S][/M][/A][/D:mm-dd-yy]
```

The first group of parameters refers to the source file(s), whereas the second set of parameters specifies the target file(s). The parameters in this command have the following meaning:

d: This specifies the disk drive. The drive specifications differ between DOS 2.X and 3.X:

DOS 2.X—Unless the user's system has a second hard disk, the first drive specification in the command is C. If the system has only one floppy disk drive, the second drive specification is A. Note that the second drive specification (the target drive) *must* be included in this command.

DOS 3.X—The source and target drives can be of any type. That is, files can be backed up from a fixed disk to a fixed disk; from a diskette to a diskette; from a fixed disk to a diskette; and, from a diskette to a fixed disk.

path   This designates a specific directory in the directory hierarchy where the file or files to be copied are located. If no path is specified, then the current directory is used.

filename   A single file may be designated. More than one file may be specified through the use of global filename characters. When this parameter and the .ext parameter (the filename extension) are omitted, all files in the designated directory are copied.

.ext   This specifies the filename extension. Global filename characters are permitted.

/S   When this parameter is included in the command, BACK-UP also copies the files in all subdirectories below the directory level specified in the path parameter. Thus, if the path parameter specifies the root directory, this parameter causes all files in the directory system to be copied. This is called a full backup.

/M   This parameter should be used only after one full backup has been performed. When this parameter is included in the command, only files that have been modified since the last backup are copied.

/A   DOS normally erases all the existing files on a diskette before it starts copying files under the BACKUP command. This does not happen when the /A parameter is included in the command. It causes the backup copies to be added to a diskette's existing files.

/D:mm-dd-yy   When this parameter is included, only files that have been created or modified on or after the specified date are copied. For example, if backups are needed only for files modified or created on or after June 30, 1984, this parameter is written as /d:6-30-84.

Note: With DOS 3.X, the parameter [d:][path] may be placed in front of the command. Since BACKUP is an external command, this allows the user to specify the particular drive and directory in which the command file is located. The pathname is separated from the command by a backslash (\).

Procedures for Making a Complete Backup

Before a complete backup is made of all files on the fixed disk, the user should have enough formatted diskettes available to accommodate all the files on the fixed disk. To determine roughly how many diskettes will be needed, the CHKDSK (Check Disk) command can be used to find out how many bytes the fixed disk is using. Then divide this number by 360,000, or the approximate number of bytes that can be stored on a floppy diskette. The result should be roughly the number of diskettes that will be used during the backup. For a 10MB disk filled to capacity, at least 28 diskettes would be required for a complete system backup.

If the user's system has one fixed disk drive and one floppy disk drive, the following command would begin the backup process:

BACKUP c:\ a:/s

A second fixed disk drive (D) and/or a second floppy disk drive (B) could be substituted in the command for the source and target drives (C and A), if this is applicable to the user's system.

Notice that there must be a space between the source and target drive specifications. The /S parameter causes all subdirectory files to be copied in addition to the root directory files. After this command is entered, DOS prompts the user to insert a diskette. If the first diskette cannot hold all the files on the fixed disk, DOS will prompt the user to insert another one. The first one should be removed and labelled "1." This process continues until all the files have been copied. It is important that the diskettes are numbered in the order in which they are used. As each file is backed up on the floppy diskette, its name is displayed on the screen.

Figure 10–6 shows the type of information that is displayed on the screen when only the root directory is backed up (the /S parameter is not included in the command).

```
C>backup c:\ a:

Insert backup diskette 01 in drive A:
Warning! Diskette files will be erased
Strike any key when ready

*** Backing up files to diskette 01 ***
\IBMBIO.COM
\IBMDOS.COM
\COMMAND.COM
\CONFIG.SYS
\AUTOEXEC.BAT
\MODE.COM
\INSTALL.DOC
```

Figure 10–6. Screen display generated when only the root directory is backed up (/S parameter not included in BACKUP command).

It is a good idea to have two separate sets of backup diskettes. If a power or system failure occurs before the backup routine is completed, all the backup files are useless. This is because BACKUP erases everything on the floppy diskette. When the program is interrupted, the previous backup is destroyed before the new one is completed. The user should alternate between two sets of diskettes whenever a complete or partial backup is performed. This ensures that both sets are current.

Procedures for Making a Partial Backup

After a complete backup has been performed, the user has the option of creating backup copies of only those files that have been created or modified since the last backup was made. There are several ways to do this:

1. **Using the Filename Parameter.** By including the filename in the BACKUP command, the user can specify that only certain files are to be copied. For example, the command

   ```
   backup c:budget1.wks a:
   ```

   creates a backup only for a file named BUDGET1.WKS. Global filename characters can be used in the filename parameter. This command, for example, copies all the spreadsheet files in a designated subdirectory:

   ```
   backup c:\123files\*.wks a:
   ```

2. **Using the /D (Date) Parameter.** The /D parameter can be used to selectively backup fixed disk files that have been created or modified on or after a specified date. However, this means that the user must keep track of the date on which the last full backup was done. Suppose that date is August 27, 1985. The following command creates floppy backups of all files modified or created on or after that date:

   ```
   backup c:\ a:/d:8-27-85
   ```

   DOS examines each file's date stamp to determine if it meets the criterion specified in the BACKUP command. For this reason, it is important that the date is entered each time the system is turned on. Since DOS and many applications program have AUTOEXEC.BAT files that include the DOS DATE and TIME commands, this is an easy task.

3. **Using the /M (Modify) Parameter.** When this parameter is included in the BACKUP command, DOS creates backups of only those files that have been created or modified since the last backup. DOS is able

to tell whether a file has been modified or if it is a new file by examining a certain bit in each file's directory entry. When a copy of this file is made with the BACKUP command, this bit has an "on" status. Whenever a file is created, or whenever a file is modified, this bit is given an "off" status. In the following command, all files on the fixed disk that are new or have been modified since the last backup will be copied:

```
backup c:\ a:/s/m
```

10.4. Using the RESTORE Command

The RESTORE command is used to place one or more files copied by the BACKUP command back onto the fixed disk. If a file is accidently destroyed, it may be recreated with this command if it has been copied onto a floppy diskette with BACKUP. If a fixed disk has failed, this command restores the BACKUP copies after the repair. Note that files copied with the BACKUP command can be used only after they have been placed back onto the fixed disk with RESTORE.

However, BACKUP and RESTORE do not have to be reserved for solving or preventing data loss problems. For example, suppose a user wishes to transfer the contents of an entire subdirectory to another fixed disk. When many files are involved, or when some of the files might be too large to fit onto floppy diskettes, the BACKUP command is used to make the duplicates. The RESTORE command is then used to place the floppy backup files onto the other system's fixed disk.

The Format of the RESTORE Command

The RESTORE command is entered in the following format:

```
RESTORE d: [d:][path][filename][.ext][/S][/P]
```

Note: With DOS 3.X, the parameter [d:][path] may be placed in front of the command. Since RESTORE is an external command, this allows the user to specify the particular drive and directory in which the command file is located. The pathname is separated from the command by a backslash (\).

The meaning of the different parameters in this command is as follows:

d: This specifies first the source drive and then the target drive. In an XT or AT with a single fixed disk drive and a single floppy disk drive, these parameters are specified as A and C, respectively. Note that the source drive *must* be included in the command.

path	The directory to which the file or files are to be restored is specified by this parameter. Files are restored to the current directory if no path is specified.
filename	This parameter allows specific files to be restored to the fixed disk. Global filename characters may be used to designate more than one file. If no filename or filename extension is specified, then all files in the directory are restored.
.ext	This designates the filename extension. Global filename characters are permitted.
/S	All subdirectories below the directory level specified in the path parameter are restored when this parameter is included in the command.
/P	When this parameter is included in the command, DOS displays a prompt before restoring files that have been changed since the last backup, or files that are marked Read-Only.

Restoring All Fixed Disk Files

If a complete system backup has been performed, the following command restores all the backup copies on the floppy diskettes to the fixed disk:

```
restore a: c:\/s
```

DOS prompts the user to place the first backup diskette into the floppy drive. After this is done, pressing a key causes the operation to begin. If the system backup used more than one diskette, DOS pauses and prompts the user to insert each numbered diskette in turn. The diskettes must be restored in the correct sequence; if not, DOS will pause and display an error message. The operation will resume only when the correct diskette is placed in the disk drive.

If partial backups have been made since the last full backup, the full backup should be restored first. Then—beginning with the oldest—the partial backups should be restored. This process adds to the fixed disk all those backup files that have been created or modified since the last full backup. If the fixed disk contains new files that are not on the backup diskettes, they are not erased. Unlike the BACKUP command, RESTORE does not erase files on the disk before copying the backup files from the floppy diskettes.

Performing Partial Restorations

Suppose a user has made a complete backup of all the fixed disk files, but has made no partial backups for the files that have been created and/or modified since the last full backup. The /P parameter of the RESTORE command allows the user to choose whether or not to restore those files that have been modified since the full backup. This is accomplished by entering the command as:

```
restore a: c:\/s/p
```

The /S option is included so that all subdirectory files will be restored along with the root directory files.

Specific files or groups of files may be restored by using the filename and filename extension parameters. For example, the following command restores a file called TRAVEL.DOC into a subdirectory named WP:

```
restore a: c:\wp\travel.doc
```

Global filename characters can be used to restore groups of files:

```
restore a: c:\123files\*.wks
```

The above command restores all the backup files in a subdirectory called 123FILES that have filename extensions of .WKS.

10.5. Automating the DOS Backup Routine with Batch Files

Batch files can greatly simplify the backup process. This can be especially important when individuals whose skill level or motivation to perform system backups is not high. Some batch files are descibed below that perform various types of backup routines. The process of backing up data can be simplified even more when backup batch routines (such as the ones described below) are incorporated into a user-designed menu. Chapter 12 demonstrates how these concepts can be incorporated in a menu system.

A Complete System Backup Batch File

This batch routine performs a complete system backup. The user only needs to enter the batch file name and have the appropriate number of diskettes ready. The commands contained in this batch file are described below:

—————————————————— *Example 10–10.* ——————

```
echo off

echo

echo This routine performs a complete system backup.

echo You must have formatted diskettes ready.

echo To abort, press [Ctrl] [Break]. Otherwise . . .

pause

path c:\utility

backup c: a:\/s
```

The first line of this batch file turns off the display of the batch file commands. The second ECHO is used to place a space between the ECHO OFF command and the messages that follow; its "text" consists of space characters. Unless these space characters are used, the system will display the message "Echo is off."

The next four lines display messages. The PATH command in the seventh line is useful because BACKUP is an external command. BACKUP is not a command that is loaded into the RAM memory when the computer is turned on; it is stored on a disk. In this example it is stored in a fixed disk subdirectory called UTILITY. The BACKUP command cannot be executed unless the current directory contains the BACKUP command file. However, the PATH command tells DOS to search in the UTILITY directory for any command or batch file not found in the current directory.

The last line of Example 10-10 begins the backup process. Figure 10–7 shows the resulting screen display up to the PAUSE command. This batch file is called FULLBACK.BAT.

```
C>fullback

C>echo off

This routine performs a complete system backup.
You must have formatted diskettes ready.
To abort, press [Ctrl] [Break].  Otherwise . . .
Strike a key when ready . . .
```

Figure 10–7. Screen display generated by FULLBACK.BAT (through the PAUSE command). Striking any key resumes the batch file.

A Backup File with Replaceable Parameters

The same batch routine described above can be modified slightly so that it can be used for both partial and complete backups. The main modification occurs in the line containing the BACKUP command. A batch file that could be used for both full and partial backups is described below:

─────────────────────── **Example 10–11.** ───────────────────────

```
echo off

path \utility

backup c: a:\%1%2
```

This makes the batch file far more versatile. The two replaceable parameters in the command (%1 and %2) are specified when the batch file is executed. Suppose that this batch routine is now called PARTBACK.BAT. The following command will backup only those files in the directory system that are new or have been modified since the last backup:

```
partback /s /m
```

Observe that spaces (or commas) must be placed between the /S and /M parameters. The next command creates a backup only for the files in the 123FILES subdirectory:

```
partback 123files
```

Notice that the second replaceable parameter does not have to be specified; DOS simply ignores it in the batch file if it has not been specified in the command line.

The batch file shown in Example 10–11 could be preceded by a separate batch routine that displays explicit instructions. This approach is useful for individuals not experienced in batch or backup routines. For example, suppose a user begins a backup procedure by calling up a batch file named "BACKFILE.BAT." This activates the batch file shown in Example 10–12:

_____*Example 10–12.*_____

```
echo off

cls

echo        ******************** INSTRUCTIONS **********************

echo

echo        To backup only those files that have been created or

echo           modified since the last backup, enter the following

echo           command:

echo                                partback /s /m

echo

echo        To backup files in only one directory, for example,

echo           the WP directory, enter the following command:

echo                                partback wp

echo

echo        To backup ALL the files on the fixed disk, enter the

echo           following command:

echo                                  fullback

prompt ENTER BACKUP CHOICE:
```

The gaps between the ECHO commands and the text are designed to center the messages on the screen. The ECHO commands that are used to separate the three messages (i.e., they have no text) must use space characters as "text" when being entered in EDLIN. Figure 10–8 shows how the screen display appears when the above batch file is activated.

```
*************************INSTRUCTIONS*************************

    To backup only those files that have been created or modified
        since the last backup, enter the following command:
                            partback /s /m

    To backup files in only one directory, for example,
        the WP directory, enter the following command:
                            partback wp

    To backup ALL the files on the fixed disk, enter the
        following command:
                                fullback
    ENTER BACKUP CHOICE:
```

Figure 10–8. Screen display generated for backup file routine.

10.6. Data Backup Using External Hardware

A user's data backup needs may go beyond the security provided by copying files to floppy diskettes with the DOS BACKUP and RESTORE commands. If this is the case, there are special backup devices that provide a higher level of security. These are usually external hardware devices that use either disk cartridges or tape cartridges as the storage medium. They differ from one another mainly in terms of reliability, speed, and capacity. This section provides a brief summary of some of the options that are available for individuals who may need this type of data security.

Although these devices are almost all external, this is changing. A growing number of manufacturers have microcomputers with special backup devices built into the system unit.

Removable Disk Cartridges

These products generally consist of a hard disk drive that uses removable disk cartridges. The cartridges usually hold 5 to 10 megabytes of data. Like the fixed disk on the XT or AT, these hard disk drives are very fast. Making a full backup is a straightforward process because the entire contents of the fixed disk can be copied quickly onto the disk cartridge.

In addition to their speed, another advantage of disk cartridges is that the computer may read the data directly from the disk cartridge after the backup has been made. There is no need to restore the files to the fixed disk before they can be used.

There is some debate about the reliability of these storage devices when compared with that of removable tape cartridges (discussed below). It has been said that disk cartridges are susceptible to dust and shock. For this reason, they are not considered as safe as tape cartridges. But for speed and convenience, disk cartridges clearly have the advantage.

Removable Tape Cartridges

The basic components of these storage devices are a digital tape cartridge drive and removable digital tape cartridges. The cartridges can hold from 10 to 40 megabytes of data. However, these devices are considerably slower than systems using removable disk cartridges. It takes about the same amount of time to backup the fixed disk on a digital tape cartridge as it does using floppy diskettes. Also, it is necessary to restore the tape backup copies to the fixed disk before they can be used. In spite of the slow speed, it is considerably more convenient than backing up a hard disk with floppies because the procedure can be started and then left unattended.

Tape drives may be either *non-streaming* or *streaming:* A non-streaming tape drive reads or records data on the tape only when the computer tells it to do so. After the task is completed, it stops until it is given another command; a streaming tape drive, on the other hand, moves its tape past the read/write heads continuously. The computer must be able to read or supply data as fast as the drive moves. Most digital tape cartridge drives are of the streaming variety. Streaming tape drives are better suited for backup purposes because they are mechanically simpler. This makes them more reliable because they are less likely to break down. Streaming tape drives also are less expensive.

Digital tape cartridges are generally considered to be more reliable storage devices than disk cartridges. They also have much larger storage capacities than disk cartridges. However, the trade-off is that a backup done with removable tape cartridges is considerably slower and less convenient than a backup done with disk cartridges.

10.7. Software- and Hardware-Controlled Security

In many areas of business, controlling system access and data duplication is just as important as protection against irreparable data loss. Previously in this chapter, some DOS routines were described that could be used for these purposes. However, the minimum-level security afforded by those routines may not be adequate for some users.

This section provides an overview of the types of security that may be obtained by special security-oriented packages. The products discussed here cover three different areas of security: access control, copy protection, and audit trails. Some security packages attempt to cover all of these areas; others may specialize in only one or two. Furthermore, there are products that use only software to provide security in these different areas. Other products use both hardware and software to accomplish this.

This area of the microcomputer industry is changing rapidly. New products are introduced frequently. For this reason, no products are discussed here by name. This discussion is intended to give the reader a general idea of what types of security packages are currently available. For the most up-to-date information on specific products, the reader should contact the Association of Data Processing Service Organizations (ADAPSO); this group has set up a clearing house for information on hardware and software products that address the problems of microcomputer data security and software piracy.

Types of Security Available

Listed below are the different areas of microcomputer security for which products are available:

1. Access Control. Certain products allow a user to restrict data and system access. Using sophisticated password systems, an individual can be "locked out" of the system entirely. Or, a user may be permitted access to some programs and data files but not to others. Further, a user may be permitted to read particular data files, but not to write to them. Each level of access in such a hierarchy is controlled through the use of passwords. Generally, there is a master password for the system manager that permits access to all levels.

2. Audit Trails. It also is possible to keep track of who has used a system. This is known as an audit trail. Security packages with highly developed access control often have schemes that pair a password with a specific user. Each time the password is used, it may be recorded in a special file, together with the date and time of its use. Thus, a manager can keep track of both when and by whom the system and/or specific files have been used. This type of system can be particularly useful when many individuals must use a system that contains important or sensitive data.

3. Copy Protection. There are products available that prevent unauthorized duplication of programs or data stored on the fixed disk and floppy diskettes. Files or programs may be encrypted with a special code that prevents them from being copied. Other encryption programs may allow information to be copied, but only onto specially encrypted diskettes; the diskettes themselves may not be copied. This type of system can prevent illegal duplication of applications software that is not copy-protected (such as dBASE II). In such cases, the programs are copied onto encrypted diskettes. The users are then given these diskettes to run the programs rather than the original program diskettes. For organizations concerned about their liability for illegal software duplication, security packages of this type may be worth considering.

Software-Only versus Software-Hardware Packages

The various systems described above may consist only of software or both software and hardware. The systems using hardware devices usually require the installation of a special board or chip in the system unit of the XT or AT. The differences between software-only and software-hardware systems generally reflect differences in cost and vulnerability.

Software-hardware systems are usually more expensive, but are less vulnerable to "cracking." Any system that consists only of software for enforcing its security may be vulnerable to penetration by another software package. This is particularly relevant to programs that perform data encryption as a form of copy protection. Prime examples of this are the popular word processing and spreadsheet packages that are vulnerable to commercially available software programs designed to break copy protection schemes.

When copy protection is the object, systems that use a DES chip in the system unit are considered superior to those that simply imitate DES with software only. DES, which stands for *Data Encryption Standard*, was developed by IBM. It involves installing an extra chip in the system unit. It is the most widely used form of data encryption, and it is usually invulnerable to penetration.

The above discussion is not meant to suggest that adequate security can be achieved only with programs that use both hardware and software. The nature of the data stored on the XT or AT and the work environment determine how much security is appropriate; in many situations, software-controlled security may be all that is necessary. Also, there are many who believe that no security package is invulnerable. Probably anyone with the technical expertise, equipment, persistence, and motivation can break most security systems. Fortunately, individuals posesssing all of these traits are fairly uncommon.

Other Security Devices

There also are security devices available that are principally of an anti-theft nature. Through the use of bolts, racks, or mounts, computer equipment can be attached to a desk or table top. Removing the equipment may require considerable effort. Similar devices also may control the use of the equipment with special cards or keys.

A number of companies market workstations in which the major components of the system may be locked away. A thief must break into the workstation to gain access to the computer. The computer is physically secure without being permanently attached or bolted to a desk or table top.

As mentioned previously, the Keylock on the AT can also be purchased for the XT and the PC. The lock is installed over the power switch on the sytem unit.

10.8. A Summary of Information on Security

1. The AT comes with a physical security device that locks the keyboard. Physical security devices can also be purchased for the XT and the PC.
2. Simple security prevention routines can be installed on a hard disk system using DOS commands. A password batch file may be written, or files can be made to appear hidden.
3. With DOS 3.X, the ATTRIB command can be used to protect sensitive files from inadvertent erasure.
4. The DOS BACKUP and RESTORE commands are used to produce duplicate copies of data files. These routines should be used whenever data files are updated. The user may perform either a complete system backup or one of the following partial backups: specified files may be backed up; files may be backed up by date; or only those files that have been modified since the last backup are included.
5. Special backup devices that provide a higher level of security can be purchased. These include removable disk cartridges and removable tape cartridges.
6. It is thought that removable tape cartridges are more reliable than removable disk cartridges. However, the disk cartridges are faster and more convenient.
7. Tape devices may be either non-streaming or streaming. Streaming tape devices are thought to be more reliable and less expensive.
8. Security packages that cover access control, copy protection, and audit trails can be purchased.
9. Differences between software-only and hardware-software security devices generally reflect differences in cost and vulnerability. Software-hardware devices are usually more expensive but less vulnerable.

11.

Thinking Ahead to Networking

At some point in the process of developing individual XT or AT workstations, the system manager may have to deal with the larger issue of linking together otherwise separate workstations. The basic motivation for this linkup is to facilitate the sharing of resources. In the data processing world, networking means sharing—sharing data, sharing programs, or sharing hardware.

The purpose of this chapter is to introduce the reader to the subject of PC networks. The objective here is not to cover all of the technical details of networks; the intent is to provide enough basic information so that one may fully understand what a network can do, and what issues are involved in setting up a PC network.

When approaching networks for the first time, one point should be kept in mind: It is not necessary to be conversant in all of the technical details of local area networks to make the correct decision on the most appropriate network for one's organization; it is important only that one know enough to ask the right questions about each possible network.

11.1. Some Information about Networks

Local Area Networks (LANs) generally refer to privately owned networks that provide high-speed communication among information processing equipment. This equipment is located in a limited geographic area such as an office, a building, or a complex of buildings. A network of IBM PCs permits one PC workstation to share data, programs, and/or hardware with another PC in the network. The hardware might be a laser printer, a modem, a fixed disk, or any other peripheral device that is available at one workstation in the network but not at another.

This section introduces the reader to the important components of PC networks and to some of the critical issues that he or she will confront in selecting a network. The characteristics of PC-to-PC networks are described, along with the nature of the network software. Also discussed are the media, topology, speed, and other terminology.

PC-to-PC Networks

Although many components of the data processing environment can be shared in LANs, PC-to-PC networks differ from other LANs in one regard: In general, they usually do not share processing. That is, the microprocessor of one PC is not shared among a number of different users; instead, each work-station (or *node*) in the network is equipped with its own microprocessor (i.e., a CPU). In contrast, in a network with shared processing, the terminal of each user does not have processing capabilities of its own and relies on a host machine; this type of network is thought of as a *multiuser network*. Until recently, shared processing was far more typical in minicomputer and main-frame networks than in microcomputer networks. Use of the AT in multiuser networks is discussed later in this section.

Network Servers

Most PC networks are structured around special computers whose princi-pal function is to service the network tasks and commands. These computers are known as *servers*, and they are the heart of the network. The server can be used in many different ways, depending on the nature of the network. It is important to understand the different types of servers because, in many respects, the server has a more important role in determining the nature of a PC network than any other component of the network.

The most important distinction in describing network servers is whether the server is a *disk server* or a *file server*. The distinction between the two often determines the speed, security, and flexibility of the network. The hardware is basically the same for both types; it is the network software that generally determines whether the server is a disk server or a file server.

Disk and File Servers

Disk servers are less complicated than file servers. In most cases, the disk server functions simply as an additional hard disk that is shared by each station on the network. Each station may be assigned a separate portion of the server's disk space. Generally, only one station at a time may use a server's file. File servers, on the other hand, are found in more sophisticated networks. They are much faster because the network software is in control of each workstation. Workstation commands are processed by the network operating system first. Less memory at the local level is required to run a network with a file server. A single file may be shared simultaneously by separate stations. If the network has stations using different operating systems, some file servers permit file sharing among stations not using the same operating system.

Dedicated and Non-Dedicated Servers

Servers also are described as being *dedicated* or *non-dedicated*. A dedicated server performs no other tasks besides its network functions. The dedicated server is not used as a separate workstation. Some networks may use special dedicated servers that have faster microprocessors than those found in the XT or AT. A non-dedicated server acts as both a network server and an individual workstation on the network itself. Its microprocessor and disk share time and space with network tasks and its local workstation activities. The speed of a workstation that is also functioning as a network server may be substantially reduced.

Centralized and Distributed Servers

Still other terms applied to the server are *centralized* and *distributed*. A centralized-server network has a single server as the physical center of the network. Each station in the network is connected directly to the server. In a centralized-server network, it is generally easier to control security. However, when the server goes down, the entire network may be disabled. Also, in some centralized-server networks only the disk and hardware resources of the server may be shared; the resources of the stations may not be directly available to one another. Distributed-server networks consist of one or more machines functioning as the server. When all stations function as servers equally, this type of distributed network is sometimes called a "peer network." In this type of configuration, each station may share the data and hardware resources directly with another station in the network. Such networks are less vulnerable to system failure than centralized-server networks.

Network Software

In selecting a PC network, it is important to consider the network software carefully. A network's ease of use, flexibility, and security are all affected by the network software. All networks must use some special software. This software may be simple or complex, depending on the nature of the network. It generally operates in tandem with the operating system software of each station in the network.

Network software often contains separate modules that perform different functions. For example, many networks contain separate print spooler programs that are essential for sharing a network printer. These spooler programs may be quite elaborate. Network software also may include special communication programs, which may permit communication with large mainframe computers. Other popular communication features frequently found in network software are electronic message systems. These facilities allow a station on the network to send messages to other stations on the network and to receive and store them as well. Some electronic mail systems include complete text editors.

It also is common to find network software that provides RAM-disk and disk-caching capabilities. A RAM disk is an area in RAM that is set aside as a temporary electronic disk drive. It is used as a temporary storage medium for the retrieval of data or files, just like another disk drive (except that it disappears when the computer is turned off). Because it is electronic rather than mechanical, a RAM disk is much faster than a hard or a floppy disk drive. Disk caching stores the most recently used file in memory. When a program frequently reads a particular file from disk, disk caching can be useful if that frequently-read file is stored on the server. A station using a network's disk caching may read the file from its memory rather than from the network server. Use of a RAM disk and disk caching can significantly speed up a network's performance time.

Network security also is a function of the network software. The amount of data security provided by the software can vary greatly. The use of password protection, file locking, and logon IDs are common features in the software of many networks.

If these features are important considerations in selecting a network, then it is essential to investigate thoroughly the capabilities of the software.

11.2. Some Network Terminology

Any discussion of networks with systems professionals is generally loaded with buzzwords and jargon. It is easy to feel overwhelmed. This is unnecessary because there are really only a few areas of networking where a knowledge of the terminology is necessary. This section presents some of the fundamental concepts and terms with which the reader should be familiar.

Topology

Topology simply refers to the way the network is connected. It determines the path that information takes when it moves from one point to another on the network. A network's topology affects a system's reliability, cost, and the ease with which maintenance and expansion may be performed on the system. There are three basic types of network topology: star, ring, and bus. Although there are other variations, they are derived from these three types.

Figure 11–1 shows a diagram of the star, ring, and bus network configurations.

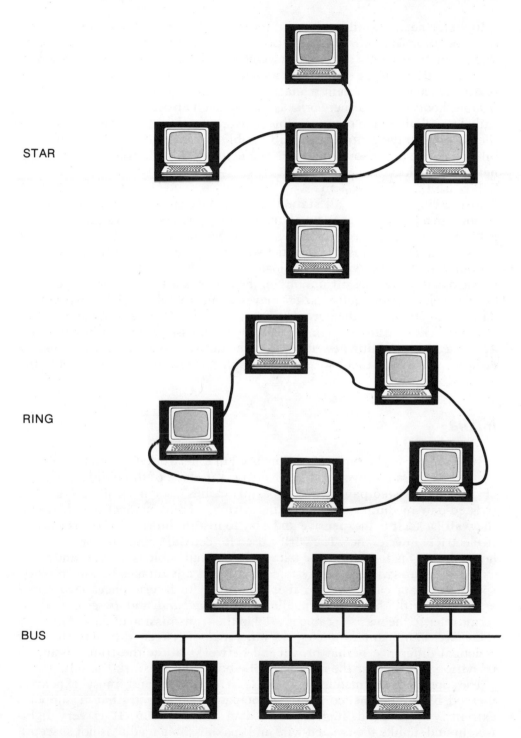

STAR

RING

BUS

Figure 11–1. Local Area Network topologies.

In a star network, all stations on the network are connected to a central point or hub. This hub may be a central computer or a connecting device that is in turn linked to a central computer. All network information is routed to this central point. One advantage of star networks is that it is relatively easy for a system manager to perform network maintenance and troubleshooting on star networks. However, such an arrangement is intrinsically less reliable than other possible network topologies because a failure in the network at the central point will disable the entire network. When reliability must be an important feature of a network, it is desirable to look for a network topology that has no *critical node*—a point at which a malfunction will crash the whole system.

In the ring topology, all stations on the network are connected to one another in a kind of ring. Network information passes from station to station around the ring. This type of network topology requires the least amount of cabling. Expansion of this type of network may be more complicated than in networks with other types of topologies.

The bus topology has all stations on the network attached to a single cable or channel. Network information moves along the channel in a stream of data. Each station on the network shares the bus with the other stations on the network for transmission, and listens for messages on the bus that are addressed to it. Adding new stations to the network is relatively simple in a network with a bus topology, since new stations are simply hooked onto the bus.

Media

Media refers to the types of cabling used in a network. Cost and flexibility are the basic issues involved here. Networks use one of three different types of media: twisted-pair wires, coaxial cables, or optical fibers. The twisted-pair medium is similar to the wiring used to connect telephones to the wall jacks. It is inexpensive and easy to install, but it can be susceptible to electrical interference. The wiring used for coaxial-cable networks is similar to the wiring used for cable television. Coaxial cable is heavier and more expensive than twisted-wire systems, but it has advantages in transmission speed and data capacity, and it is less prone to interference. Two terms associated with the coaxial medium are *broadband* and *baseband*; these terms refer to the way the cable is used in the transmission of data. Although there are significant technological differences between the two, the only practical difference is that broadband networks allow the transmission of television signals over the network while baseband networks do not.

The optical-fiber medium is the least common and most expensive method of cabling networks. Its principal advantage is that it supports extremely high-speed, high-capacity data transmission. It is very lightweight and, unlike the twisted-wire and coaxial-cable media, is not susceptible to electrical interference.

Access Protocols

Protocol means rules. *Access protocols* refer to the rules that regulate network access by the individual stations. It is not particularly essential that one be familiar with this subject when making decisions about a PC network. Nevertheless, some of the more common access protocols are described here because it is not unusual to encounter this subject in discussions or literature on networks.

Access protocols can be divided into two groups. One group uses methods described as *contention techniques*, whereas the other group uses *non-contention techniques*. These two groups are discussed below.

Non-Contention Techniques

These types of access protocols allow network access by individual stations in a predetermined order. These techniques prevent conflicts (collisions) by regulating access to the network. Access protocols of this type are often described as polling techniques; that is, individual stations on the network are asked in turn, "Do you wish to transmit?"

One particularly common polling technique that is often used in ring networks is *token passing*. A *token* is simply a special data set that is passed around the network from station to station. When a particular station has possession of the token, it may transmit a message. The message is attached to the "empty" token with the network address of the receiver. Until the token is again empty, no other station may transmit.

Contention Techniques

Contention techniques anticipate conflicts because no predetermined order is defined for giving stations network access. Access is regulated by anticipating conflicts before and during transmission. When conflicts do occur, specific procedures are then followed.

One contention technique that is particularly popular in PC networks is *Carrier Sense Multiple Access/Collision Detection* (CSMA/CD). This protocol regulates the usage of the network line without any one station controlling when transmissions may occur. It operates in the following way: When a station wishes to transmit, it listens to the network line until the line is clear of any other network traffic; this is the "Carrier Sense" portion of the CSMA/CD protocol. However, if two stations begin transmitting simultaneously, both thinking that the line is clear, then a collision occurs. Both stations immediately cease transmission and wait a short, randomly determined length of time before attempting to re-transmit. This is the "Collision Detection" portion of CSMA/CD. The CSMA/CD protocol is typically found in distributed bus networks.

Multiuser Networks

In a multiuser network, the microprocessor of one PC is shared among a number of different users. The terminal of each user does not have processing capabilities of its own, but instead relies on a host machine. Each station simply functions as a dumb terminal. Until recently, shared processing was far more typical in minicomputer and mainframe networks than in microcomputer networks using the IBM Personal Computer as the host. The PC-AT's microprocessor, the Intel 80286, allows it to be used as the host machine in a multiuser network. A section of the 80286 microprocessor (the memory management unit) allows an operating system or other software to strictly control segments of memory for specific tasks. A task might be a user in the network or, if it is a single-user system, the task could be one of several programs being run concurrently. (Note: This latter feature is not supported by DOS 2.X or 3.0/3.1.)

11.3. Decision Issues

There are a number of factors that should be considered in choosing a PC network. Each organization will have its own needs, so the issues that are important will vary from one organization to another. The nature of the network—its design, topology, media, and software—should be determined by which of these factors are the most critical. The issues that are important to an organization will automatically narrow the choices.

This section outlines some of the key issues that should be considered.

What Will Be Shared?

If the purpose of a network is to share resources, then one should begin by identifying those resources that must be a part of the network. This is a critical issue. There are significant differences among the various PC network products. The strength of one network may be its ability to share hardware; another might be better suited for sharing programs and data.

When the primary function of the network is to share peripheral devices, it is important to note that the types of devices that may be shared vary widely among the multitude of PC networks. Most networks permit serial and parallel printers to be shared; however, far fewer permit the sharing of modems. Other devices that might be shared include plotters, hard disk drives, tape drives, and RAM disks. A network product may allow some of these devices, but not others, to be shared.

There also is a great deal of variability found in the file sharing capabilities in the different PC networks. Some off-the-shelf software packages may not work well or may not run at all on a particular network. It is advisable to investigate or try out the program under multiuser conditions if at all possible. This is especially true for database programs that involve the sharing of a large database. If many users must frequently add, delete, or edit information in a database file, the network must provide sufficient controls so that the integrity of the database can be maintained. Most networks provide some type of disk sharing, file locking, or record locking schemes to protect data that is being accessed simultaneously. (Note, however, that very few database packages support locking and sharing.) How much control is necessary depends on the size of the system. A small system with five users is not going to require the same kind of file sharing controls necessary in a network of 30 users.

Does the Network Have To Be Fail-Safe?

The reliability of the network involves its vulnerability to system failure. This often is a function of the network server. The number of servers in a network can be an important factor. Just as the hard disk of a stand-alone PC-XT and AT is vulnerable to failure, so too is the hard disk of a network server. Spreading the network files among more than one server (a distributed server network) decreases the vulnerability of the data. If one server fails, network files might be accessed at a different location. The nature of the data stored on the server should determine whether a centralized- or a distributed-server network is more appropriate for an organization's needs.

The topology of the network also can affect the network's reliability. Consideration should be given as to how a failure in the server affects the performance of the rest of the network. What happens to the stations on the network when the server is down? Are they able to continue communicating with each other? Is it necessary that they be able to do so? The star network, with its complete dependence on a centralized server, is the least secure type of network topology in this respect; if the server fails, the entire network may be disabled. On the other hand, a distributed bus network offers the most reliability because if one station fails, the rest of the network activity may be able to continue without interruption.

What Are the Security Needs?

Network files can be vulnerable to unauthorized access. Access restrictions for information stored on a network server are usually controlled through network software. The levels of security provided by different PC networks can vary greatly. Although data can be physically more secure in a distributed network, it should be noted that it is generally easier to control access to the data in a centralized-server network.

In most PC networks, access restrictions typically are handled through the designation of specific files or volumes (partitions) on the network server as public, private, or shared. Public files or volumes are accessible to all users on the network. A public file may be Read-Only for all except perhaps a system manager or the file's "owner." Files and volumes designated as private or shared may be given password protection. Access to that file or volume then is permitted only when a user knows the correct password. Private and shared files and volumes might be Read-Only or read/write.

In the most extensive security systems, there are several levels of access: The first level of security restricts network access with password protection; the next level may determine what type of activities a user may perform on the network, such as reading files, writing to files, creating or deleting files, and so on; another level of security may restrict the volumes or directories to which a user has access. Finally, a user may be restricted to using only specific files.

Public and shared files that are designated as read/write are especially vulnerable to corruption when several users are attempting to write to a file simultaneously. In some systems, data protection is ensured by simply "locking" the file when it is in use. When the shared file is a large database that is constantly being changed by many users, this type of system may not be appropriate. More sophisticated systems may have record locking facilities that flag only specific records in a file. However, both file locking and record locking utilities may be dependent upon the application program in order to work. If this is an important issue, it is wise to investigate a network's capabilities thoroughly in this regard. It may be necessary to run a program on the network to see how it works when a read/write file is written to and saved simultaneously by more than one user.

What Are the Expansion Requirements?

It may be necessary to add stations and devices to the network at some later time. It is important to examine both the ease with which this can be accomplished and the limitations of specific networks. Distributed bus networks generally have the most flexible expansion capabilities. Consideration also should be given to the total number of users that ultimately will be hooked into the network. PC networks have widely differing capabilities in the number of workstations that they support: Less expensive networks tend to support only 15 to 30 stations, while some of the more sophisticated products provide support for hundreds of workstations.

In addition to adding more workstations, it also may be necessary to add more servers to the network. Again, there are differences in the capabilities of the various network products. Some of the more popular PC networks do not allow more than one server. In other networks, more than one server may be used, but there may be limits on the number of stations allowed per server.

PC networks also have differing memory requirements for the individual workstations. Most network stations usually require a memory capacity of 128K to 256K. The memory requirements for a server are generally higher.

How Sophisticated Are the Users?

Ease of use should be considered from the perspective of both the users and the system manager. From the end user's point of view, the functionality of the network should be as transparent as possible. In some networks, most of the operations performed by users are executed through menu-driven programs. This can be particularly important if many of the users are not accustomed to keying in commands at an operating system level. When the level of sophistication of the users is not particularly high, it may be important that the system have some kind of on-line HELP screens. A good set of HELP screens can be far more useful than even the most clearly written documentation.

Ease of use does not concern just the end user; the ease with which system management functions can be performed should be a consideration in any network buying decision. The system manager will be regularly required to set up volumes and directories on the server, assign security status to various volumes and files, and perform backup routines. Depending on the size of the system, it also may be important that the network have appropriate diagnostic software for troubleshooting in the servers, workstations, and cabling.

Will A Printer Be Shared?

If sharing a printer is an important function of the network, then it would be wise to make sure that a network's printer-related software is adequate for the needs of the users. Most PC networks include special programs for printing called *print spoolers*. Basically, a print spooler allows a user to send a document to a printer, regardless of whether or not the printer is already in use. If the printer is busy with another document, then the new document is temporarily stored and is put into a queue. The document is printed when its turn comes in the queue.

As might be expected, there is a great deal of variability in print spooling software: Some spoolers allow documents in the queue to be reordered or they allow the queue to be emptied; other features may permit a document to be deleted from the queue or permit multiple copies to be made of a file in the queue. Spoolers can be disk-based, RAM-based, or both. Disk-based spoolers store documents in the queue on disk; RAM-based spoolers store files in the queue in memory. If it is expected that a shared printer will have heavy usage, then it may be important to consider networks whose print spoolers are disk-based. The advantage of such programs is that a large printing operation would not have to be rerun if the network failed before the job was completed.

It also is important to make sure that the type of printers used are supported by the network. Not all printer models will necessarily run on a given network. Finally, it should be noted that some networks require that a shared printer be attached to a server. This means that any printer that is attached to a user workstation cannot be shared.

Other Hardware Issues

There are a number of installation factors that will automatically narrow the choices among the various PC networks. The number of users is one such factor: Many networks have limitations on the number of stations that can be hooked into them. Another factor is the physical distance that is to be covered by the network. Different networks have different limitations on the maximum distance allowed between workstations: The range can be anywhere from 2,000 to 20,000 feet.

There also are specific memory requirements for both the workstations and the servers on the network. The amount of memory necessary will vary, depending on the vendor. The memory requirements for a server tend to be higher.

If sharing data or programs is an important function of the network, then consideration also should be given to the amount of data that will be stored on the server. Obviously, if the amount of information exceeds the storage capacity of a 10- or 20-megabyte fixed disk, then the system will require either more than one server or a special server with a larger fixed disk capacity.

Is Cost an Issue?

For the most part, other issues will predetermine the costs of a PC network. For example, if the network must serve 40 users and have a high degree of reliability, flexibility, and security, then one can assume that such a system, no matter how it is to be configured, is not going to be cheap. However, there are some components of a network where costs can be controlled to a certain degree.

If it is not essential to have a dedicated server, one can lower costs significantly by using one or more stations on the network as the server. Implementing the network becomes less expensive because no investment is made in buying the server computer. The trade-off is that the performance time of the workstation functioning as the server may be significantly reduced. This may not be a viable option if heavy server usage is expected.

Another area where costs can be controlled is in the network media (i.e., the cabling). Twisted-pair wiring is considerably less expensive than coaxial cable. A number of popular PC networks use this medium. The trade-off here is that twisted-pair wiring has limitations in terms of both data capacity and transmission speed.

One area of the network that is not dependent on other issues is the cost of the network per workstation. Each PC in the network will require a network adapter card. The cost of the card may vary greatly from one network to another. This is particularly relevant if it is expected that more stations will be added to the network at a later time.

In comparing costs of different networks, it must be noted that different networks may have different hardware and cabling requirements. Probably the simplest way to compare costs among the different network vendors is to look at the bottom-line costs involved in setting up a network with a specific number of workstations. It also is a good idea to look at how the costs increase comparatively as the number of workstations and the physical distances expand.

11.4. A Summary of Information on Networking

1. A local area network (LAN) of PCs permits one PC to share data, programs, and/or hardware with another PC in the network. The hardware might be a laser printer, a modem, a fixed disk, or any other peripheral device included in the network.
2. PC-to-PC networks differ from LANs in that workstations in networks do not share processing; each workstation is equipped with its own CPU.
3. Network servers are computers whose principal function is to service network tasks and commands. They may be disk servers or file servers (the network software generally determines whether the server is a disk server or a file server). Disk servers are simpler, but file servers are faster and require less memory at the local level.
4. Servers may be dedicated or non-dedicated. A dedicated server performs only network functions; i.e., it is not used as a separate workstation.
5. Servers may be centralized or distributed. A central server is physically located in the center of the network. Each station is directly connected with it. Distributed-server networks use one or more machines as the server. Security is easier to control with central servers, but distributed servers are less susceptible to failures.
6. Topology refers to the way that the network is connected. A network's topology affects system reliability, cost, and ease of maintenance and/or expansion. There are three types of topologies: star, ring, and bus.
7. Media refers to the type of cabling used. This affects the cost and flexibility of the network. Media may be twisted-pair wire, coaxial cables, or optical fibers.

8. Access protocols refer to the rules that regulate network access by individual stations. There are two groups of access protocols: those using contention techniques and those using non-contention techniques.

9. Multiuser networks are networks in which the microprocessor of one computer is shared among a number of different users. The AT's microprocessor, the Intel 80286, allows the AT to be used as the host machine in a multiuser network.

10. When choosing a network, one should consider the following: What will be shared (files or devices); whether or not the network must be fail-safe; what security features are required; whether or not and how the network must expand; the sophistication of the users; and the cost of the network.

12.

A Sample Menu
Management System

A sample Menu Management System is presented in this chapter. It includes four main features:

1. a batch file password entry system
2. a Main Menu and Submenu System
3. HELP Screen facilities
4. a System Messages Board for leaving and updating user messages on the system.

The password entry system is activated from within the AUTOEXEC.BAT file when the system is booted. This password system utilizes display-attribute control codes to restrict access to the main menu unless a password is entered. The remaining features of this disk management system are listed as menu options in a Main Menu screen. Choosing any one of these options activates a batch file. These batch files then produce submenu screens (e.g., Software Submenu). The first selection in each submenu is always the choice, "Return to Main Menu." This activates a batch file that loops the user back to the starting point. Thus, this feature prevents the need to either reboot the system or to repeat the password access process. A schematic diagram of the sample Menu Management System is presented in Figure 12–1.

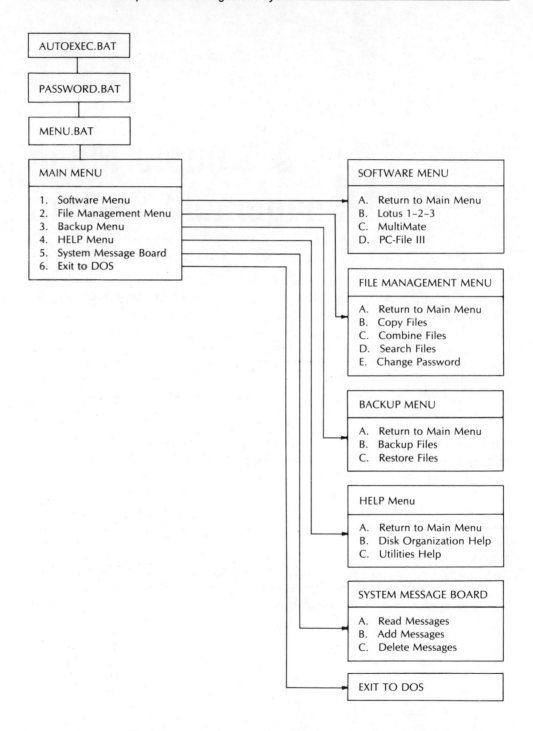

Figure 12–1. Schematic diagram of the sample menu management system.

This system was designed using many of the systems management techniques discussed throughout the book. All of these techniques are implemented using the operating system. Batch files are used to create each of the menu/submenu options. DOS's hierarchical directory structure is used as a basis for the hierarchical menu structure. The user screens are created using EDLIN and DOS's ASCII graphics capabilities. Modification of the display screen (e.g., masking of the password) is accomplished by activating attribute-specific escape sequences from within batch files.

It should be noted that this menu system is designed to be run on either the XT or the AT. Thus, those features that may be desirable for an XT system (e.g., password-protected menu access) may not be necessary for an AT-based system. In addition, enhancements to DOS in version 3.X may not be available to the DOS 2.X owner. Thus, the following menu systems may be constructed using either DOS 2.X or 3.X. The DOS 3.X owner may want to modify or enhance this system by using DOS 3.X features such as VDISK (a virtual RAM disk), or directory and path specifications for external DOS commands.

The approach taken in this chapter is to present and describe the following components of the system:

1. A copy of each user screen.
2. The batch files executed by each menu selection.
3. The results (or in some cases, a sample result) produced by each menu selection.

12.1. The Password System

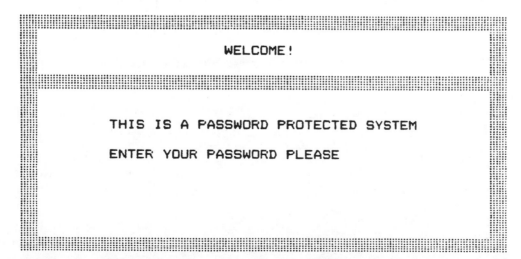

Figure 12–2. Password screen as it appears on the screen.

Display of the password screen (see Figure 12–2) is activated from within the AUTOEXEC.BAT file. If a color monitor is being used, the batch file can produce a color screen and mask the password by producing the same foreground and background colors. For monochrome displays, the password can be masked by making the foreground invisible. Both color and monochrome display alternatives are presented.

Color

AUTOEXEC.BAT

echo off	Turns off DOS command display
type blue.scr	Changes background to BLUE
cls	Full screen area becomes BLUE
type password.scr	Password screen (Figure 12–2) is displayed
type blue.car	Masks password (characters are BLUE)

Monochrome

AUTOEXEC.BAT

echo off	Turns off DOS command display
cls	Clears (blanks) screen
type password.scr	Password screen (Figure 12–2) is displayed
type display.off	Turns off screen display

The user must respond to the password screen by typing the correct password. This password is the name of a batch file that displays the Main Menu screen.

PASSWORD.BAT

echo off	Turns off DOS command display
type display.on	Restores screen display to normal
type menu.scr	Displays the Main Menu
prompt ENTER SELECTION:	Prompts user for selection

12.2. The Main Menu

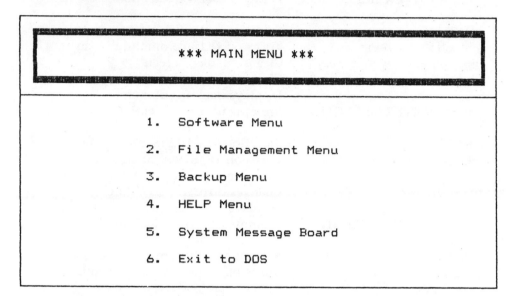

```
            *** MAIN MENU ***


        1.   Software Menu

        2.   File Management Menu

        3.   Backup Menu

        4.   HELP Menu

        5.   System Message Board

        6.   Exit to DOS
```

Figure 12–3. Main Menu screen.

The Main Menu (see Figure 12–3) serves as the entry point into the entire fixed disk system. It includes selections that 1) automatically load applications software, 2) present the user with a variety of file management utilities (including backup options), 3) make on-line HELP screens available to the user, and 4) allow the user to read, delete, or store messages on a system message board. Each of the Main Menu selections produces a submenu; the user can return from the submenu to the Main Menu at any point in time.

The Main Menu contains six options. Each of these options is a batch file that changes the directory and displays the appropriate submenu screen. The submenu screen for each menu choice is located in a separate directory. Batch files for each menu option are named 1.BAT, 2.BAT, and so on.

1.BAT	Selection 1: Software Menu
echo off	Turns off DOS command display
cls	Clears (blanks) screen
cd\software	Changes directory to C:\software
type soft.scr	Displays software submenu
prompt ENTER SELECTION:	Prompts user for selection
2.BAT	Selection 2: File Management Menu
echo off	Turns off DOS command display
cls	Clears (blanks) screen
cd\utility	Changes directory to C:\utility

type mgmt.scr	Displays file management submenu
prompt ENTER SELECTION:	Prompts user for selection

3.BAT	Selection 3: Backup Menu
echo off	Turns off DOS command display
cls	Clears (blanks) screen
cd\backup	Changes directory to C:\backup
type save.scr	Displays backup submenu
prompt ENTER SELECTION:	Prompts user for selection

4.BAT	Selection 4: HELP Screen Menu
echo off	Turns off DOS command display
cls	Clears (blanks) screen
cd\help	Changes directory to C:\help
type help.scr	Displays help screen submenu
prompt ENTER SELECTION:	Prompts user for selection

5.BAT	Selection 5: System Message Board
echo off	Turns off DOS command display
cls	Clears (blanks) screen
cd\message	Changes directory to C:\message
type mess.scr	Displays message board submenu
prompt ENTER SELECTION:	Prompts user for selection

6.BAT	Selection 6: Exit to DOS
echo off	Turns off DOS command display
cls	Clears (blanks) screen
cd\	Returns to Root (C:\) directory

12.3. Software Menu

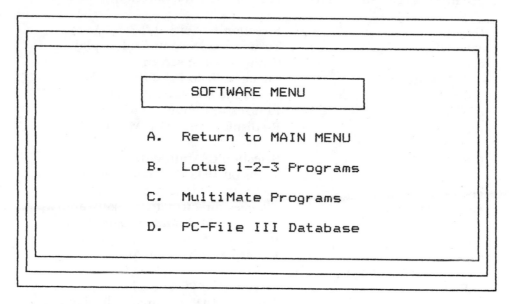

Figure 12–4. Software Menu screen.

The Software Menu (see Figure 12–4) contains selections for each type of applications software stored on the fixed disk. For example purposes, a spreadsheet package, a word processing package, and a database package are included in the software submenu. Choosing the desired selection automatically loads the software package and brings the user to the software package's own menu system. It should be noted that application software packages often contain their own AUTOEXEC.BAT file. The user may want to delete this file when creating a software submenu. Batch files for each submenu option are named A.BAT, B.BAT, and so on.

When a Software Menu selection is made, control is passed from DOS to the appropriate software package. When the user exits the software package and returns to DOS, the batch file continues execution. Thus, the last two lines of each Software Menu batch file contain a loop back to the Main Menu screen. This is automatically executed whenever the user exits the software program(s).

The following batch files supporting the Software Menu can be found in the C:\software directory:

A. BAT	Selection A: Return to Main Menu
echo off	Turns off DOS command display
cls	Clears (blanks) screen
cd\	Returns to Root (C:\) directory

type menu.scr	Re-displays the Main Menu
prompt ENTER SELECTION:	Prompts user for selection

B.BAT	Selection B: Lotus 1-2-3
echo off	Turns off DOS command display
cls	Clears (blanks) screen
cd\software\123	Changes dir to C:\software\123
lotus	Loads the Lotus 1-2-3 program
cd\	Returns to Root (C:\) directory
type menu.scr	Re-displays the Main Menu

C.BAT	Selection C: MultiMate
echo off	Turns off DOS command display
cls	Clears (blanks) screen
cd\software\wp	Changes directory to C:\software\wp
wp	Loads the MultiMate program
cd\	Returns to Root (C:\) directory
type menu.scr	Re-displays the Main Menu

D.BAT	Selection D: PC-File III
echo off	Turns off DOS command display
cls	Clears (blanks) screen
cd\software\data	Changes dir to C:\software\data
pc-file	Loads the PC-File III program
cd\	Returns to Root (C:\) directory
type menu.scr	Re-displays the Main Menu

12.4. File Management Menu

```
        ┌──────────────────────────────┐
        │    FILE MANAGEMENT MENU       │
        └──────────────────────────────┘
        A.    Return to MAIN MENU

        B.    COPY Files

        C.    ERASE Files

        D.    Search Files

        E.    Combine Files

        F.    Change System Password
```

Figure 12–5. File Management Menu screen.

The File Management Menu (Figure 12–5) provides the user with five different utilities. These include: copying files, searching through ASCII files for text strings, combining ASCII files, and changing the password. Further instructions for the user are contained as ECHO comments in each of the selection batch files. At the completion of each utility routine, the batch file returns the user to the File Management Menu.

The following batch files supporting the File Management Menu can be found in the C:\utility directory.

A. BAT	Selection A: Return to Main Menu
echo off	Turns off DOS command display
cls	Clears (blanks) screen
cd\	Returns to Root (C:\) directory
type menu.scr	Re-displays the Main Menu
prompt ENTER SELECTION:	Prompts user for selection

```
B.BAT                    Selection B:  Copy Files

echo off

cls

echo      ++++++++++++++++++++++++++++++++++++++++++++++++++++++++

echo                       COPY FILES

echo      ++++++++++++++++++++++++++++++++++++++++++++++++++++++++

echo      This is a routine that allows you to copy files to a

echo      floppy diskette or to another directory.

echo      ++++++++++++++++++++++++++++++++++++++++++++++++++++++++

echo      To copy a file to a floppy diskette, enter the command

echo      "FLOPPY," followed by a comma and the filename.

echo      ++++++++++++++++++++++++++++++++++++++++++++++++++++++++

echo      To copy a file to another directory, enter the command,

echo      "DIRECT," followed by a comma, the filename, and the target

echo      directory.  E.g.,

echo                  direct,budget1.wks,finance

echo      ++++++++++++++++++++++++++++++++++++++++++++++++++++++++

prompt ENTER COPY COMMAND:
```

Two batch files, FLOPPY.BAT and DIRECT.BAT, are activated when the user types the desired command:

```
FLOPPY.BAT

echo off

cls

copy c:\%1 a:
```

```
DIRECT.BAT

echo off

cls

copy c:\%1 c:\%2
```

```
C.BAT                      Selection C:  Combine ASCII Files

echo off

cls

echo    ++++++++++++++++++++++++++++++++++++++++++++++++++++++++++

echo                     COMBINE FILES

echo    ++++++++++++++++++++++++++++++++++++++++++++++++++++++++++

echo    This is a routine that permits the user to combine up to

echo    four  ASCII files.  All files can be appended in sequence

echo    to the initial/source file, or all files can be combined

echo    into a new target file.

echo    ++++++++++++++++++++++++++++++++++++++++++++++++++++++++++

echo    .....To append the files to the SOURCE file, use "APPEND."

echo    ++++++++++++++++++++++++++++++++++++++++++++++++++++++++++

echo    .....To combine files into a TARGET file, use "COMBINE."

echo    The output of COMBINE will be in a file named, "TARGET.TXT."

echo    ++++++++++++++++++++++++++++++++++++++++++++++++++++++++++

echo    Type the appropriate command followed by a comma and each

echo    of the file names to be combined.  E.g.,

echo                  append,text1.prn,text2.prn

echo    ++++++++++++++++++++++++++++++++++++++++++++++++++++++++++

prompt ENTER COMBINE COMMAND:
```

Two batch files, APPEND.BAT and COMBINE.BAT, are activated when the user types the desired command:

```
APPEND.BAT
echo off
cls
copy c:\%1 + %2 + %3 + %4


COMBINE.BAT
echo off
cls
copy c:\%1 + %2 + %3 + %4 target.txt


D.BAT                    Selection D:  Search for Strings
echo off
cls
echo    +++++++++++++++++++++++++++++++++++++++++++++++++++++++++++++
echo                      SEARCH FILES
echo    +++++++++++++++++++++++++++++++++++++++++++++++++++++++++++++
echo    This is a routine that permits the user to search through
echo    ASCII files for all occurrences of a particular string.
echo    The string for which you are searching must match identically
echo    with the search key word.....
echo    +++++++++++++++++++++++++++++++++++++++++++++++++++++++++++++++
echo    At the prompt, enter the command "SEARCH," followed by a comma
echo    and the text string for which you are searching.
prompt ENTER SEARCH COMMAND:
```

When the user issues the command "SEARCH," a batch file by that name is activated:

```
SEARCH.BAT

echo off

path c:\DOS

for %%f in (*.dat) do find /n"%1" %%f
```

The *.dat specification in the FOR command causes the FIND command to be performed on every file in the current directory having the .DAT file-name extension. The %%f functions as the dummy for each "real" file in the *.dat set. The "%1" represents the character string that is the subject of the search. Using a replaceable parameter here means that any string entered on the command line with the batch filename can be the subject of a search.

```
E.BAT                   Selection E: Change Password

echo off

cls

echo     ++++++++++++++++++++++++++++++++++++++++++++++++++++++++++++++

echo                    PASSWORD CHANGE

echo     ++++++++++++++++++++++++++++++++++++++++++++++++++++++++++++++

echo     This is a routine to change your system password. At the

echo     prompt, type the command "CHANGE" followed by the OLD and

echo     NEW passwords.  Separate the command "CHANGE," the old

echo     password, and the new password with commas.

prompt ENTER PASSWORD CHANGE COMMAND:
```

Choosing the selection "E" activates a batch file that contains instructions on the required format for changing a password. The ECHO command in the batch file tells DOS to type each line of instructions on the screen. The "prompt" command changes the prompt from C> to the text string "ENTER PASSWORD CHANGE COMMAND:". When E.BAT is activated, the following screen appears:

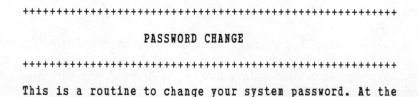

```
     ++++++++++++++++++++++++++++++++++++++++++++++++++++++++++++++

                    PASSWORD CHANGE

     ++++++++++++++++++++++++++++++++++++++++++++++++++++++++++++++

     This is a routine to change your system password. At the
```

```
prompt,type the command "CHANGE" followed by the OLD and

NEW passwords.  Separate the command "CHANGE," the old

password, and the new password with commas.
```

ENTER PASSWORD CHANGE COMMAND:

The user responds to the prompt as instructed; this activates another batch file. For example, the response:

change,giraffe,capybara

activates a batch file named "CHANGE.BAT" that has two replaceable parameters:

```
echo off

cls

prompt $n$g

rename %1.bat %2.bat

echo        New Password is: %2

echo        Pressing any key will redisplay the File Management Menu

pause

type mgmt.scr

prompt ENTER SELECTION:
```

This batch file is activated with the "CHANGE" command that the user types. The old password is the first replaceable parameter and the new password is the second. Thus, the fourth line of the batch file renames the first parameter with the name of the second parameter. The batch file then displays the folllowing on the screen:

```
New Password is: capybara

Pressing any key will redisplay the File Management Menu
```

Strike any key when ready...

The new password name "capybara" is automatically inserted after the text "New Password is:". The PAUSE command allows the user to verify that the new password is correct. Then, when any key is pressed, the File Management Menu is automatically displayed.

12.5. Backup Menu

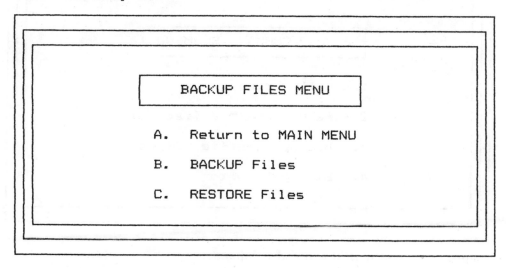

Figure 12–6. Backup Menu screen.

The File Backup Menu (Figure 12–6) provides the user with options for backing up and restoring files. The following batch files supporting the Backup Menu can be found in the directory C:\backup:

A. BAT	Selection A: Return to Main Menu
echo off	Turns off DOS command display
cls	Clears (blanks) screen
cd\	Returns to Root (C:\) directory
type menu.scr	Re-displays the Main Menu
prompt ENTER SELECTION:	Prompts user for selection
B.BAT	Selection B: File Backup Submenu
echo off	Turns off DOS command display
cls	Clears (blanks) screen
type save1.scr	Displays a BACKUP command submenu
prompt ENTER SELECTION:	Prompts user for selection

Selection B, The BACKUP command submenu, displays four options for the user (see Figure 12–7). These choices include the following tasks:

1. Performing a full backup
2. Backing up only new or modified files
3. Backing up files in a specified directory
4. Backing up all files created or modified after a specified date.

```
┌─────────────────────────────────────────────────┐
│ ┌─────────────────────────────────────────────┐ │
│ │                                             │ │
│ │      ┌─────────────────────────────┐        │ │
│ │      │  BACKUP  COMMAND  SUBMENU   │        │ │
│ │      └─────────────────────────────┘        │ │
│ │                                             │ │
│ │      1.   Full Backup                       │ │
│ │                                             │ │
│ │      2.   Backup New/Modified Files         │ │
│ │                                             │ │
│ │      3.   Backup Specified Directory        │ │
│ │                                             │ │
│ │      4.   Backup By Date                    │ │
│ │                                             │ │
│ └─────────────────────────────────────────────┘ │
└─────────────────────────────────────────────────┘
```

Figure 12–7: BACKUP Command Submenu.

The following batch files support the BACKUP command submenu and are located in the C:\backup directory:

```
1.BAT                   Selection 1:  Full Backup
path c:\DOS
backup c:\ a:/s


2.BAT                   Selection 2:  New/Modified Files
path c:\DOS
backup c:\ a:/s/m


3.BAT                   Selection 3:  Specified Directory
echo off
cls
echo         +++++++++++++++++++++++++++++++++++++++++++++++++
echo             SPECIFY DIRECTORY TO BE BACKED UP
echo         +++++++++++++++++++++++++++++++++++++++++++++++++
echo         This routine backs up a specified directory.  At
```

```
echo         the prompt, type the command "SAVE," followed by

echo         the name of the directory.  Separate the command

echo         directory name with a comma.

prompt  ENTER DIRECTORY SAVE COMMAND:

save.bat
```

This batch file (3.BAT) activates a batch file named "SAVE.BAT" when the "SAVE" command is typed. This batch file contains the following commands:

path c:\DOS

backup c: a:\%1

The directory name typed by the user becomes the replaceable parameter (%1).

```
4.BAT                    Selection 4:  Backup By Date

echo off

cls

echo         +++++++++++++++++++++++++++++++++++++++++++++++++++

echo                  SPECIFY EFFECTIVE DATE FOR BACKUP

echo         +++++++++++++++++++++++++++++++++++++++++++++++++++

echo         This routine backs up all files modified or

echo         created after a specified date.  At the prompt,

echo         type the command "SAVEDATE," followed by the date.

echo         The format for the date is MM-DD-YY.  Separate the

echo         command and the date with a comma.

prompt  ENTER DATE COMMAND:

savedate.bat
```

This batch file (4.BAT) activates a batch file named "SAVEDATE.BAT" when the "SAVEDATE" command is typed. This batch file contains these commands:

```
path c:\DOS

backup c: a: /d:%1
```

The date typed by the user becomes the replaceable parameter (%1).

C.BAT	Selection C: Restore Command
echo off	Turns off DOS command display
cls	Clears (blanks) screen
type replace.scr	Displays a RESTORE command sub-menu
prompt ENTER SELECTION:	Prompts user for selection

Selection C, The RESTORE command submenu, displays two options for the user (see Figure 12–8). These choices include the following tasks:

1. Restoring all files
2. Prompting the user with names of files that have changed since the last backup

```
┌─────────────────────────────────┐
│  RESTORE COMMAND SUBMENU  │
└─────────────────────────────────┘

  1.   Restore All Files

  2.   Prompt User With Changed Files
```

Figure 12–8. RESTORE Command Submenu.

The following batch files support the RESTORE command submenu and are located in the C:\backup directory:

```
1.BAT               Selection 1:  Restore All Files
path c:\DOS         Specifies path to DOS External Commands
restore a: c:\/s    Restores all subdirectories



2.BAT               Selection 2:  Restore Prompt
path c:\DOS         Specifies path to DOS External Commands
restore a: c:\/s/p  Restores all subdirectories and prompts
                    user before restoring files that have been
                    changed since the last backup
```

12.6. Help Screens

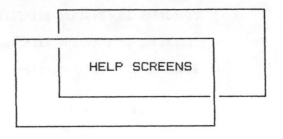

```
        A.   Return to MAIN MENU

        B.   Disk Organization HELP

        C.   File Management HELP
```

Figure 12–9. HELP Screen Menu.

The HELP Screen Menu (Figure 12–9) in this example contains two different HELP options: Disk Organization HELP and Utilities HELP. HELP Screens are created using any text editor. Then, they can be displayed "on-line" with the TYPE command. By passing the files through the MORE filter, the display of the text pauses after each screen is filled. The user presses any key to continue the display.

The following batch files supporting the HELP Screens Menu can be found in the C:\help directory:

A. BAT	Selection A: Return to Main Menu
echo off	Turns off DOS command display
cls	Clears (blanks) screen
cd\	Returns to Root (C:\) directory
type menu.scr	Re-displays the Main Menu
prompt ENTER SELECTION:	Prompts user for selection
B.BAT	Selection B: Disk Organization HELP
echo off	Turns off DOS command display
cls	Clears (blanks) screen
path c:\DOS	Specifies path to DOS External commands
type disk.txt ¦ more	Types text; places MORE command in text

pause	Pauses at the end of the HELP text
cls	Clears (blanks) screen
echo off	Turns off DOS command display
type help.scr	Re-displays the HELP Screen Menu
prompt ENTER SELECTION:	Prompts user for selection
C.BAT	Selection C: Disk Organization HELP
echo off	Turns off DOS command display
cls	Clears (blanks) screen
path c:\DOS	Specifies path to DOS External commands
type utility.txt ¦ more	Types text; places MORE command in text
pause	Pauses at the end of the HELP text
cls	Clears (blanks) screen
echo off	Turns off DOS command display
type help.scr	Re-displays the HELP Screen Menu
prompt ENTER SELECTION:	Prompts user for selection

The screen displays generated by B.BAT and C.BAT show approximately 20 lines of text and the message:

`-- More --`

at the bottom left of the page (see Figure 12–10). When the user presses any key, the next screen is displayed.

```
                    PATH Command HELP

  1. If no disk drive is specified for a path, the current drive is
     used.
  2. More than one directory path may be specified in the PATH
     command; each must be separated by a semicolon.
  3. It is a good idea to always start paths from the root
     directory.  If the root directory is not the starting point in
     a path, DOS assumes that the path begins with the current
     directory.  This may result in an invalid path.
  4. Any path that contains invalid information (such as a bad
     drive name or a nonexistent directory) will be ignored.
  5. Only program command files and batch files are affected by
     the PATH command (i.e., files with filename extensions of
     .EXE, .COM, or .BAT).
  6. The PATH command can be most useful when it is included in
     an AUTOEXEC.BAT file.  This file type is automatically
     executed when a system or program is booted.  For example, the
     DOS 2.00 disk contains an AUTOEXEC.BAT file that automatically
  -- More --
```

Figure 12–10. HELP Screen as it appears on the display screen.

12.7. System Messages

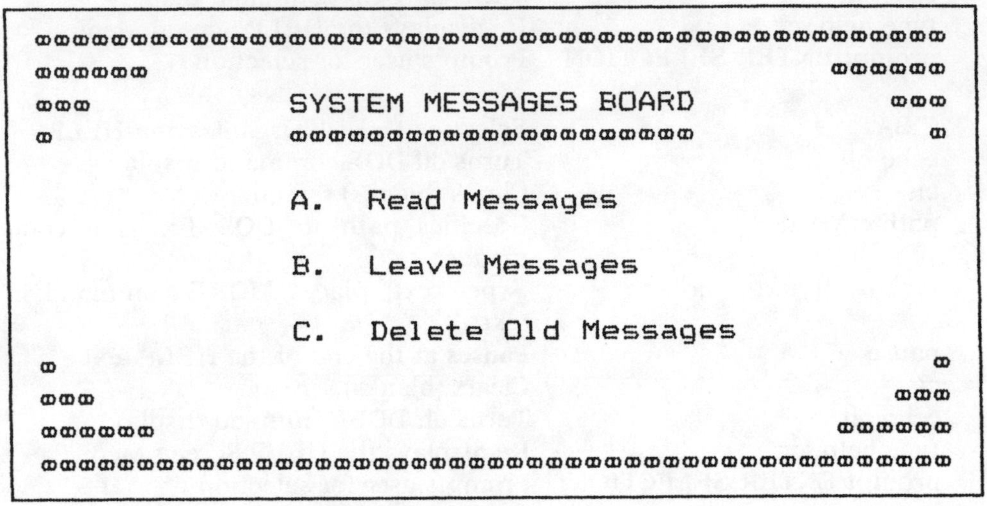

```
∞∞∞∞∞∞∞∞∞∞∞∞∞∞∞∞∞∞∞∞∞∞∞∞∞∞∞∞∞∞∞∞∞∞∞∞∞∞∞∞∞∞
∞∞∞∞∞∞                                          ∞∞∞∞∞∞
∞∞∞              SYSTEM MESSAGES BOARD              ∞∞∞
∞              ∞∞∞∞∞∞∞∞∞∞∞∞∞∞∞∞∞∞∞∞∞∞                ∞

               A.   Read Messages

               B.   Leave Messages

               C.   Delete Old Messages
∞                                                      ∞
∞∞∞                                                  ∞∞∞
∞∞∞∞∞∞                                          ∞∞∞∞∞∞
∞∞∞∞∞∞∞∞∞∞∞∞∞∞∞∞∞∞∞∞∞∞∞∞∞∞∞∞∞∞∞∞∞∞∞∞∞∞∞∞∞∞∞∞∞∞
```

Figure 12–11. Message Board Screen.

The System Message Board (Figure 12–11) allows the user to read messages, leave messages, and delete old messages. Each message is a separate file. When the message board is read, a file containing all of the messages is displayed. This file is called SYSTEM.BRD. Initially, two versions of the SYSTEM.BRD file must be created. One file is located in the C:\messages directory. Although this file at first contains nothing more than a few space characters, it must already exist before any messages can be added to it. The second SYSTEM.BRD file is located in another directory. Although it too is empty except for a few blank spaces, no messages are ever added to it; it is used only when the message board is to be completely erased.

The following batch files supporting the System Message Board can be found in the C:\messages directory.

```
A.BAT                      Selection A:  Read Message Board
echo off
cls
echo     +++++++++++++++++++++++++++++++++++++++++++++++++++++++++++++
echo                     READ MESSAGE BOARD
echo     +++++++++++++++++++++++++++++++++++++++++++++++++++++++++++++
pause
type system.brd | more
cd\
type menu.scr
prompt ENTER SELECTION:
```

This file types out the contents of the System Board that contains all the individual message files. The MORE filter displays one screen of messages at a time.

```
B.BAT                      Selection B:  Leave Messages
echo off
cls
echo     +++++++++++++++++++++++++++++++++++++++++++++++++++++++++++++
echo                     LEAVE A MESSAGE
echo     +++++++++++++++++++++++++++++++++++++++++++++++++++++++++++++
echo     Instructions:
echo     To start the message routine, type the word "ADD" followed by
echo     your initials and a message number.  E.g.,
echo          ADD,NC1        This is for the first message
echo          ADD,NC2        This is if you already have one message
echo                            on the board
echo     Be sure to enter the date in the body of the text message
prompt ENTER MESSAGE COMMAND:
```

When the user enters the command "ADD," it activates a batch file by that name:

```
ADD.BAT

echo off

cls

echo      Enter your message now.....

echo      Press the F6 key and [ENTER] when done.....

copy con: %1.txt>NUL

copy system.brd + %1.txt>NUL

cls

echo      Message added to System Board.
```

This batch file creates a message file from the information that the user types on the screen. This message is then added to the file named SYS-TEM.BRD. The >NUL symbols at the end of the COPY commands suppress the display of the DOS message "1 File(s) copied."

```
C.BAT                 Selection C:  Delete Message(s)

echo off

cls

echo      ++++++++++++++++++++++++++++++++++++++++++++++++++++++++++++++

echo                      DELETE MESSAGE(S)

echo      ++++++++++++++++++++++++++++++++++++++++++++++++++++++++++++++

echo      +++++                                              +++++

echo          1.  Erase all messages

echo          2.  Erase selected messages

echo      +++++                                              +++++

prompt ENTER SELECTION NUMBER:
```

When the user enters either a "1" or a "2," a batch file by that name is activated:

```
1.BAT

echo off

cls

echo      Erasing all messages.....

erase *.txt

copy \utility\system.brd \messages>NUL

echo      All messages erased.
```

This batch file erases all messages and then uses the COPY command to replace the SYSTEM.BRD file in the C:\messages directory with the empty SYSTEM.BRD file located in the C:\utility directory. The >NUL after the COPY command suppresses the display of the DOS message "1 File(s) copied."

```
2.BAT

echo off

cls

echo                    Message Deletion Options

echo      +++++++++++++++++++++++++++++++++++++++++++++++++++++

echo      To delete ALL messages enter the command "REMOVE,"

echo      followed by your initials and an *

echo      For example:   remove,NWC*

echo                     remove,TC*

echo      +++++++++++++++++++++++++++++++++++++++++++++++++++++

echo      +++++++++++++++++++++++++++++++++++++++++++++++++++++

echo      To delete a SPECIFIC message, enter the command

echo      "REMOVE," followed by the initials and message #.

echo      For example:          remove,nwc1

echo      +++++++++++++++++++++++++++++++++++++++++++++++++++++

prompt  ENTER REMOVE COMMAND:
```

When the user types the command "REMOVE," a batch file by that name is activated:

```
REMOVE.BAT

echo off

cls

echo      Removing messages.....

for %%x in(%1,txt) do erase %%x

copy \utility\system.brd \messages>NUL

for %%a in(*.txt) do copy system.brd + %%a>NUL

echo      System Message Board is now updated.
```

The first FOR command in the above batch file erases a specific file; the second FOR command recopies out the System Message Board with the messages deleted.

Appendix A

Adding Memory to the System

Many users purchase a system and later decide to enhance the hardware. One of the most common enhancements is additional memory. The original system also may come unassembled; i.e., the user may have to install additional memory cards or memory chips. Although computer memory has several different components, memory expansion generally refers to only one type of computer memory: RAM.

Why Increase the RAM?

There are several reasons why users increase the amount of the RAM on their system. In spreadsheet programs such as 1-2-3, the size of the RAM allows larger worksheets to be used. Some software packages require a large amount of RAM just to run the program. For example, Framework by Ashton-Tate requires 384K of RAM, and Lotus Symphony requires 320K of RAM.

Another advantage of increased RAM is that extra memory often can be used as an electronic disk drive. This is particularly true for the AT, which can have up to 3MB of RAM. Depending on the RAM capacity, the computer can be told that the extra RAM is a disk drive. This electronic disk drive can be used for temporary data storage. When RAM is used in this way, it is generally called a RAM disk or virtual disk. It is useful in programs that frequently must read various sections of the program from a disk: Some of these sections can be loaded into the RAM disk, thereby making program execution considerably faster; this is because the mechanical process of retrieving information from a disk drive is far slower than the electronic retrieval from RAM.

Yet another advantage of extra RAM is that many memory-expansion boards come with software that allows the extra memory to be used for print spooling. This process uses the extra RAM to store information that is being printed. It frees the main RAM and the rest of the computer for other tasks while the data are being printed.

Installing Additional RAM

RAM may be added to the XT and AT in two ways: One method involves installing additional integrated circuit memory chips; these are placed on the system board of the system unit. The XT's system board may hold up to 256K of memory; the AT's system board can hold twice that amount, since integrated circuit chips on the AT's system board are 64K chips piggybacked into 128K chips. The other method of increasing RAM requires the installation of a RAM card or a multifunction board; both of these processes are discussed below.

Adding RAM Chips

If a user wishes to increase the memory of his or her system beyond the standard amount (256K for the XT and the Basic AT), the system board first must be filled. Memory can be added to the XT system board in increments of 64K. Thus, the XT's system board memory may be increased to either 192K or 256K, which is the maximum amount of memory that it can contain. Once the XT's system board is at capacity, RAM cards or multifunction boards can be added to the system unit to increase the XT's memory beyond 256K—usually to 640K.

Memory can be added to the AT system board in increments of 128K, up to 512K. AT memory expansion options include a 128KB memory expansion option, a 256KB memory module kit (IC chips installed by the user), and 512KB expansion options. RAM cards or multifunction boards can be added to the system unit to increase the AT's memory to up to 16MB.

The chips that are added to the system board can be obtained from a variety of sources: IBM sells them, and they also can be purchased at computer stores and mail-order houses. Indeed, the AT's 256KB Memory Module Kit is a set of 18 128K chips (a 128K chip in this kit is in fact composed of two 64K chips, in which one chip is fastened onto the top of the other). Additions to the XT are made with 64K chips; these 64K chips are sold in sets of nine, because it takes nine of them to constitute 64K of memory. (If the reader is wondering how nine chips equals 64K, the reason is that there is a chip for each of the eight bits contained in a byte, and one extra chip for error checking.)

The following steps are used to install chips on the system board:

1. Integrated circuit memory chips are very sensitive to static electricity; therefore, when handling these chips, RAM cards, and multifunction boards, the user should avoid environments that tend to increase

the buildup of static electricity in the body, such as carpeted rooms. The user should be grounded before handling the chips. Static electricity can damage and ruin the chip's circuits.

2. Disconnect the power sources on the system unit and any of the peripherals before removing the cover on the system unit.

3. Remove the screws on the rear panel of the system unit that secure the cover to the chassis.

4. Pull the cover forward until it is nearly off; then, lift the cover up slightly to free it from the front panel of the system unit.

5. The sockets for the RAM chips are located on the "floor" of the system unit, near the front left corner of both the AT and XT. The locations are identified on the system board by the following labels:

XT 'Bank 0', 'Bank 1', 'Bank 2', and 'Bank 3'
AT 'Bank 0', and 'Bank 1'

Banks 0 and 1 already contain chips on older versions of the XT; Banks 2 and 3 on these machines are empty; if only 64K of memory is being added, the chips are placed in Bank 3. On the Basic AT, Bank 0 contains 256K and Bank 1 is empty.

6. It may be necessary to remove any adapter cards that are obstructing access to the memory banks. The cards are held in place by a single screw at the back of the system unit; after this screw is removed, a card may be pulled out of its socket. This should be done with care; one should hold these adapter cards by their edges only.

7. Be sure that the pins on the chips are straight. Select the first chip for installation; it does not matter which one, since they are all identical.

8. There is a small notch or dot on one end of the chip; this identifies that end as the "Pin 1" end of the chip. Examine the chips already installed on the system board. It will be observed that the "Pin 1" ends of those chips all face the same direction. Make sure that the chips being installed also face this direction.

9. Place the chip over the socket. Tilt the chip very slightly so that the row of pins on one side edges into its holes, and then gently push the pins on the opposite side into their holes. Once both sets of pins are positioned over their socket holes, push the chip down firmly into its socket. The chip must be pushed down so that its housing touches the socket. Make sure that all pins are in the socket.

10. Repeat this process for the remaining chips on the system board.

11. Note: The XT system board contains a small set of switches; these switches must be reset so that the XT will recognize the additional memory. Consult the XT IBM Guide to Operations for the correct switch settings corresponding to the amount of memory being installed.

12. Replace any cards that have been removed, the system unit cover, and the screws securing the cover.

Adding RAM Cards or Multifunction Boards

Once the memory banks on the system board have been filled to capacity (256K on the XT or 512K on the AT), additional RAM can be added by installing a RAM card or a multifunction board. For example, a memory option for the AT is the AT 512KB memory expansion option. This is an adapter card that is inserted in an available slot. Up to five of these cards can be added to the AT to increase RAM to 3MB. In contrast, multifunction boards typically combine a parallel or serial printer interface with other features such as additional RAM and/or clock-calendars. They are useful because they enhance the computer in several ways, but use only one of the available expansion slots in doing so.

Here are some points to keep in mind when installing multifunction boards:

1. Be sure to read the instructions accompanying the boards.
2. Be sure to set the switches on the card, if there are any, before inserting the card in the system unit. Consult the documentation that accompanies the cards for the correct switch settings.
3. When choosing a slot for the card in the system unit, any available on the XT may be selected; however, the two slots behind the XT's disk drive cannot hold full-length cards. The AT's 128KB and 512KB memory expansion options can be installed in slots 2 through 8.
4. After the card has been installed, replace the system unit cover and recable the system. However, before replacing the screws at the back of the system unit, turn on the system and observe the screen values shown during the Power-on Self-Test. If any error messages are displayed, or the amount of installed RAM does not match the screen values, the switch settings may be incorrect. In this case, disconnect the power and recheck the switch settings.
5. Errors in memory are designated by the number 201. This number will be displayed on the screen during the Power-on Self-Test if there are problems. Additional four-digit numbers displayed with the 201 value indicate the location in the memory banks of one or more defective chips. The documentation accompanying the boards generally provides a guide to interpreting these numbers.

Appendix B

Moving a Hard Disk System

An XT or an AT is a reasonably durable piece of equipment while it is sitting on a desktop. This is not necessarily the case, however, when it is being moved. The disk drives are particularly susceptible to damage if proper precautions have not been taken. One of the principal causes of fixed disk problems is the user's failure to adequately prepare the computer for relocation.

All fixed disk files should be backed up before the computer is moved, even if it is only a short distance. Normal shipping and handling may result in permanent loss of the data stored on the fixed disk. The procedures for performing a system backup are described in Chapter 10.

Short Distance Moving

Any distance that does not involve transporting the equipment in a vehicle such as a car or truck might be considered a short distance. For example, moving the computer down a floor or across the hall could be considered a short move.

The steps listed below should be followed in preparing the computer for the move:

1. The procedure begins by placing the Diagnostics diskette (found in the Guide to Operations) in the floppy disk drive. A system startup or reset then should be performed, displaying the menu shown in Figure B–1.
2. Option 3, PREPARE FIXED DISK FOR RELOCATION, should be selected. The following message then is displayed:

    `FIXED DISK(S) READY FOR SHIPPING`

    (Option 3 on the AT's Diagnostic Menu is PREPARE SYSTEM FOR MOVING. After this choice is selected, the message displayed is SYSTEM PREPARED FOR MOVING.)

3. Remove the Diagnostics diskette and turn off the system.
4. The various components of the computer now can be disconnected and moved to the new location.

```
The IBM Personal Computer DIAGNOSTICS
Version 2.00 (C)Copyright IBM Corp 1981, 1982

SELECT AN OPTION

0 - RUN DIAGNOSTIC ROUTINES
1 - FORMAT DISKETTE
2 - COPY DISKETTE
3 - PREPARE FIXED DISK FOR RELOCATION
9 - EXIT TO SYSTEM DISKETTE

ENTER THE ACTION DESIRED
?
```

Figure B–1. Menu displayed by the IBM Diagnostics program.

Long Distance Moving

A long distance move is any relocation of the computer that involves shipping the equipment by car, truck, or other vehicle. The first three steps are the same as those outlined above for short move preparation; then, after the Relocation program on the Diagnostics diskette has been run, the user should follow these additional steps:

1. New system units usually come with a cardboard disk in the floppy disk drive: If this has been saved, or if one can be found, it should be placed in the floppy disk drive, and the drive door then should be closed; if this is not available, a scratch floppy diskette is better than nothing at all. The purpose of this is to prevent the heads of the disk drive from knocking against one another.
2. If at all possible, the system unit should be packed in the same box and packing material in which it originally came. The other components also should be well packed.

If the computer frequently is shipped long distances, the user should consider purchasing special shipping cases for the equipment. Products are available that are specially designed for the shipment of the IBM Personal Computer.

Appendix C

A Quick Reference Guide to EDLIN's Commands

Name	Command	Format	Explanation
Append Lines	A	[n]A	This command is used when the file to be edited is too large to fit into memory. The number of lines [n] is specified. These lines are added from disk to the end of the current line in the file being edited. If NO lines are specified, lines are appended until memory is 75% full.
Copy Lines	C	[line],[line],line[,count]C	Lines in a specified range (line #s in the first two parameters) are copied to a line # (the third parameter). The number of times this operation is to be performed [,count] also may be specified.
Delete Lines	D	[line][,line]D	Line #s in a specified range (first parameter to second parameter) are deleted. All line #s are renumbered accordingly. Single lines (first parameter only) or the current line (no parameters) may be specified for deletion.
Edit Line		[line]	Displays the line # and the text to be edited. Control and editing keys can then be used to alter the text. Entering a period (.) instead of a line # displays the current line for editing.
End Edit	E	E	The EDLIN session is terminated and the edited file is saved under the initially specified filename.

Name	Command	Format	Explanation
Insert Lines	I	[line]I	Permits user to insert line(s) immediately preceding the specified line [line] or the current line (.). Creation of NEW files requires that the I command be entered prior to inserting text.
List Lines	L	[line][,line]L	Types out the line #s and the text in a specified range (first two parameters). Twenty-three lines, beginning with the specified line, are displayed if only the first parameter is entered; eleven lines plus the current line are displayed if only the second parameter is entered; eleven lines before and after the current line are displayed if NO parameter is entered.
Move Lines	M	[line],[line],lineM	Lines in a specified range (line #s in the first two parameters) are moved ahead of the specified line # (third parameter). All line #s are renumbered accordingly.
Page	P	[line][,line]P	Types out the line #s and text in a specified range (first two parameters). Twenty-three lines are displayed if only the first parameter is entered; the current line plus one are displayed if only the second parameter is entered. The user can then "page" through a file, 23 lines at a time.
Quit Edit	Q	Q	The EDLIN session is terminated and the edited file is not saved.
Replace Text	R	[line][,line][?]R[string][<F6>string]	Lines in a specified range (line #s in the first two parameters) are scanned for the occurrence of a text string (first [string] parameter) and replaced with the text in the second [string] parameter. A confirmation prompt can be inserted before the replacement by including the [?] parameter. The search ends with the last line in memory if only the first parameter [line] is entered; the search begins following the current line if only the second parameter [,line] is entered; if both line parameters are omitted, lines following the current line to the last line in memory are searched. Note <F6> refers to the DOS function key setup or to <Ctrl-Z>.

Name	Command	Format	Explanation
Search Text	S	[line][,line][?]S[string]	Lines in a specified range (line #s in the first two parameters) are scanned for the occurrence of a text string [string] and the first line is displayed. A confirmation prompt to continue or discontinue searching can be displayed if the [?] parameter is included. Omissions of either one or both [line] parameters produce the same results as described above for the Replace Text command.
Transfer Lines	T	[line]T[d:]filename	Contents of a specified file ([d:]filename) are brought into the file currently being edited. These contents are placed ahead of the line # specified in the first parameter [line] or ahead of the current line (if no [line] parameter is specified).
Write Lines	W	[n]W	A specified number of lines [n], starting with line #1, are written to disk. This command is used when the file being edited is too large to fit into memory. This command is the opposite of the Append Lines command; it must be used to write edited lines to disk before loading additional unedited lines into memory.

Notations Used for EDLIN parameters:

[line] = a line number is specified OR
a # sign is entered to indicate the next available line in memory OR
a period (.) is entered to indicate the current line
[n] = number of lines
[string] = series of characters/text is entered
<F6> = DOS function key, F6, is pressed to signal end of string; ⌊CTrl-Z⌋ keys can be used as well
[?] = ? is entered to insert a confirmation prompt (a Yes/No decision alternative) in the Search/Replace operations

Index

RELATED BOOKS OF INTEREST FROM BRADY

Fasten your seat belt!

For the serious computer user who wants to soup up his PC—make it faster, more powerful, more fun—the experts at PC WORLD have a fascinating new book and software program that can make your personal computer truly personal.

Called *The Fully Powered PC* with *PC World Utilities Disk,* it takes you under the hood of your PC. It shows you how to construct your own system, how to combine many single-purpose systems, and how to call up a dozen or more applications with little more than a keystroke.

It puts you on the fast track by showing you how to put applications programs into active memory so they run faster, design menus to

guide you through systems you've created, even customize your computer to find and dial telephone numbers. It even includes public-domain software that add still more powerful features to your PC.

In other words, *The Fully Powered PC* helps you create a system that performs exactly the way *you* want it to. And isn't that why you bought a PC in the first place?

For the IBM PC, XT, AT or compatible. $39.95 at all computer stores. To order direct, call TOLL FREE: 1-800-437-4400, Ext. 807, or use the coupon below.

Simon&Schuster
COMPUTER SOFTWARE